Praise for Unbox! The Power of Mindful Thinking

(Feedback from readers like you)

Much needed book for the modern age distracted kids - and their parents. The big-picture view, the exercises, and the humorous illustrations made the concepts simple enough for my thirteen-year-old and eleven-year-old to understand! The associated exercises should be mandatory for everyone.

A beautifully illustrated book, in the genre of Exupery's The Little Prince, written with clarity and humor, on how we become victims of our own thoughts. Just like The Little Prince, it is a book written for kids and meant for adults. First time author Prithvi Raj Banerjee shows impressive clarity of thought and flair for putting complex things in enjoyable prose.

It was delightful reading a book that explains deep philosophical subjects in such a simple manner. Not only does the writer use allegorical illustrations to explain his take on the concept of "Thoughts" and how to deal with them in pursuit of the state of expanded attention, but he does so with suggested activities one can do to really come to grips with the concept.

UNBOX!
THE POWER OF MINDFUL THINKING

Think outside the Box, we say

But, where *is* the box?

UNBOX!
THE POWER OF MINDFUL THINKING

WRITTEN AND ILLUSTRATED BY

PRITHVI RAJ BANERJEE

Copyright © Prithvi Raj Banerjee 2016.
Mind-Gym Publishing
www.thoughtUnboxed.com

ISBN 978-0-9985090-6-8

First Published in the USA in 2017 by Amazon.

Hardcover edition published in December 2017

Cover Illustration by Ros Webb

Poem *The Blind Men and the Elephant* by John Godfrey Saxe

This book is not a substitute for the medical advice of physicians. The reader should regularly consult a physician in matters relating to his/her health and especially in respect to any symptoms that may require diagnosis or medical attention.

This book is dedicated to Antoine de Saint-Exupéry who helped me see the world of grown ups from a different perspective.

And to Yogani, who helped me see the world within from a different perspective.

And also to Anisha, for showing me the magical space where all perspectives merge.

CONTENTS

INTRODUCTION

When distracting mental chatter overpowers our attention, we lose our ability to perform effective and impactful actions.

This is the same chatter of thoughts that makes us think about work when we are on a vacation, or about the weekend when we are at work. We all have experienced this chatter when we lie in bed, thinking about things we were going to do the next day, next week, or sometimes even next year.

What if, I told you that there was a trick that could liberate us from this distracting mental chatter? And that through this book we would embark on a journey to experientially understand how to handle these distracting thoughts and potentially evolve *the way we think*. Will you be interested?

"Bring it on!" did I hear you say?

So let's get started right away!

In order to understand how distracting thoughts overpower our attention, we will need to first understand what *thoughts* and *attention* really are. And you may be surprised, just the way I was, by what you discover.

Only when we *experientially* understand what thoughts and attention are, can we move on to the next step: exploring the interplay between the two. This interplay between attention and thoughts determines the 'way we think' or simply, our 'thinking.'

It is important to note that though they are interrelated, 'thinking' is distinct from 'thoughts'. This distinction between thinking and thoughts holds the key to understanding the simple trick to evolve the way we think and liberate us from mental chatter.

So what *is* this trick?

Well, let us start thousands of years ago. Much before the modern age of severely restless and fragmented attention that feeds off fifteen-second news cycles, WhatsApp, Facebook, and Twitter alert.

Even those folks living in those ancient ages, surrounded by the unpredictability of life, disease, death, and weather, felt that their mental chatter made their attention restless resulting into troublesome and inefficient thinking. Through their cloud of anxiety, despair, and insecurity, they sensed that they were missing out on something. They discovered the existence of what we refer to in this book as a 'box' that gave us a partial and distorted view of reality. This box represents uncontrolled thoughts that cloud our minds.

Then a few wise ones figured out the trick to take this box out. The trick to take out the box, or to **Unbox**, forms the central theme of this book. This trick helps us to learn a new way of thinking, which we will refer to as **Mindful Thinking**.

Back in those ancient times, people did not have easy access to this trick. Most had to give up their regular life and live in communities devoted exclusively to finding ways to unbox. Today, this information is widely available. Guidance, for which you would have to travel half way around the world and devote decades of your life to get access to, is now one-click away on your Amazon account.

With all the perks of instant gratification that modern age has unleashed, instant unboxing remains as elusive as it was thousands of years ago. At least for the vast majority of us. There is no shortcut for the effort that is required to *really understand the trick* to get out of that box.

It should not be surprising that quality of our attention has changed dramatically over the last few decades. So intuitively one would think that some of the techniques that were formulated thousands of years ago may need to be adapted for the modern world?

But I was surprised to find out that the trick to get out of the box remained more or less the same across the ages. I was even more surprised to find out how simple this trick was and often wondered why this wisdom was not ubiquitous?

Then I finally realized what the reason was. What really needed to evolve was not the trick itself but the narrative around the trick to make it less confusing and more relatable in the modern world.

That, in a nutshell, is what this book attempts to do.

———⟞≈≋≋⟝———

I had believed for a long time that all 'thoughts' had the same structure.

The mysterious flash of image, sound, and emotions in an unseen and transient inner stuff, each thought seemed to have a similar mechanism in tapping on my attention.   They would materialize suddenly and unpredictably then fade away and disappear as mysteriously as they had appeared.

Then later, after I had spent a considerable amount of time experimenting with my thoughts, I found out that there were at least *two* distinct types of thoughts. I call these two 'cue-thought' and 'action-thought' in this book.

Based on these experiments I discovered that my attention had a distinct and different way of engaging with each of these two types of thoughts. And these different modes of engagement led to two distinct modes of thinking. I call these modes 'good thinking' and 'bad thinking'.

I later found out that these two modes of thinking were aligned to the latest findings in neuroscience. The Default mode Network or DMN was correlated with mental chatter and Task Positive Network (TPN) with focused attention.

Even as I continued my experiments with thoughts and thinking, I was lucky enough to be guided by masters from great mindfulness traditions in this effort. And gradually, over the years, the *big picture* about thoughts & thinking began to emerge.

And here is a quick summary of what I found.

> We can train our mind to perform **less** of inefficient and distracted thinking that I call '*Bad Thinking*' and **more** of focused, aligned and productive thinking that I call '*Good thinking*'.

This skill of balanced thinking that I refer to, as *mindful thinking* is a skill that can transform our lives in a very positive way.

With mindful thinking, we would make fewer mistakes. Our attention would not get easily distracted. We would do things that we want to do in a much better way. We would become more creative.

And here is the best part - we all can evolve the way we think at this very *moment* if we truly understand a simple *trick* that has been taught by masters across the ages.

It may be very apparent that *mindful thinking,* if my claims are correct, is an extremely useful skill to have. This book is an effort to demystify the realm of thoughts and help you learn that skill.

As I mentioned earlier, in my experiments with thoughts & thinking, I was lucky enough to be guided by masters from great mindfulness traditions. I was also guided further by a different set of masters at MIT where I specialized in systems thinking - an approach that uses the 'big picture' view to solve complex real-world problems.

So when I put together the *big picture* in this book, I incorporated learnings from both the worlds drawing inspiration from the spiritual and the scientific, but at the same time having an independent perspective based on my personal experiences.

This core wisdom, of course, has been around for ages, but I have tried to put these facts in the context of our current life using new metaphors that you will hopefully relate better to.

I wanted to touch upon one more aspect before we move on. This book will teach you the trick to evolve your thinking but in order to *know* the trick experientially – *you will need to perform the exercises and techniques that have been compiled in the book.*

In that regard, this book recommends an eight-week plan with specific exercises. These exercises are gently ramped up in the first five weeks to a stable routine.

You may want first to read all the chapters and their exercises as a first pass to get a 'map' of what we are trying to do here. You can then revisit the individual sections, exercises, and assignments, practicing them according to the daily/weekly schedule recommended. This latter step, needless to say, will make all the difference.

We all can evolve the way we think at this very *moment* if we truly understand the trick how to do so. The exercises and assignments will help us truly understand that trick.

These exercises are contemporary translations of some of the most effective tricks & techniques taught by masters across ages. A lot of these exercises are popular, but some remain obscure and hidden.

The small set of techniques included in this book should be sufficient for the serious explorers to start unraveling the mysteries of the inner-world and mastering the wonderful skill of mindful thinking.

In this revised edition the content had been re-aligned based on the feedback I received from readers and from participants of Unbox! Workshops. I hope you find these changes helpful.

I wish you all the best as you embark on this wonderful journey!

Prithvi Raj Banerjee
Boston, September 2017

WHY DO WE THINK?

Stories can throw us off our usual train of thoughts and engage us at a deeper level of understanding

Almost all of us come fitted with a Box. A Box made out of thoughts. We reinforce this box over our life as we grow up. We then ensure others around us have boxes as well - especially if these folks are our kids.

So, what happens if you wear this box around your head all the time? Just try walking around with your head stuck inside a cardboard box if you are truly inspired to find out.

And the box of thoughts can cause more trouble than an ordinary cardboard box can ever do.

Here, I have some Boxes for You

Now We will Have Fun !

It is because this particular box is invisible to the folks who wear it. So they go around falling and hurting themselves, puzzled and worried – but never suspecting that their head was stuck inside a box. And what happens when you take this box off?

"See things better?" you ask shrugging your shoulders.

"See things as they are," I reply, "and much more," I pause as you listen with attention.

This Box is the source of *Bad Thinking*, a type of thinking dominated by mental chatter. After you take the box off, needless to say, your thinking becomes more effective. In this book, we will learn fun tricks and playful exercises to help us take off this box.

We will also use simple stories and fables to explore why these tricks work in the way they do. These stories intend to engage us at a deeper level of understanding that remains untouched by mental chatter and habitual thoughts.

Let's now rewind to a fabled time when there were no thoughts. At least in the sense we humans experience them today.

———— ·⊰✽⊱· ————

L ong ago, when only living creatures on the planet lived in the ocean, there was a fish that was unlike any other fish. He was no ordinary fish because he was king of all the fish in the world.

The Kingfish ruled over the watery realm that engulfed the earth. He had everything that a fish would ever want. The best coral artisans of the Kingdom had built his palace. Master oysters decorated the grand palace with beautiful bright pearls. Famous seaweed designers crafted its fancy curtains. The palace had an invigorating water flow infused with the fragrance of fresh sea lichens. He had several queens who would admire him, looking from their coral coves, grateful for their fortune.

Then one day the Kingfish had an unknown urge to explore things beyond the ocean that he and his subjects had lived in throughout their life. He had a deep feeling that there was more to life than just eating fungus and flapping his gills.

That day the Kingfish swam out of the palace. He then swam out into the open ocean far from the comfort of currents known to him. Unknown to him, several other fish had set out on a similar journey from different nooks of the ocean. Over the years this shoal of fish started to all look different. Some had grown strange new muscles, some had their fins become thick and webbed, and some developed a weird shell on their backs.

Then one day, Kingfish found a magical place as the ocean water became increasingly bright. His fins grazed over hard earth, and he hesitated for a brief moment before sticking his head out of the water and into warm air. It was a whole new magical realm out there!

He pulled out of the water and took a deep breath filling his newly evolved lungs with warm air. He never knew that something like this existed when he was in the water. He walked along the coast as the wind blew against his face. He basked in the glow of the warm sun, smiling at the white clouds and the magnificent blue sky.

It had taken a very long time for the fish to emerge from the ocean and start crawling on the land. About four billion years since the time first living organisms appeared in the sea.

"Four Billion years. Well, that seems quite a lot" you might say.

But just wait and see what happens next.

The amphibians became reptiles who became mammals. All this while there was very little thinking in this world - mostly limited to help them to stay alive and procreate. But still, the creatures were learning. These learnings were wired in their body and passed from one generation to other. So they would learn cute things like building their nest, storing food for winter and clever tricks to attract their partners.

Not all these learnings were charming – like the bullying hermit crab that would force a weaker crab out of its shell and smugly occupy it without a trace of guilt. Or the cuckoo that would unabashedly replace the eggs of an unsuspecting bird with her own. All these learnings were passed from one generation to other coded within the structure of their bodies. The animals evolved with different forms developing into semi-apes and then apes.

It had been more than three hundred million years since Kingfish had stepped out of the ocean and the smartest creature on the planet were still apes who considered lice as comfort food.

"Three hundred million is better than four billion years. But it still seems quite a lot" you make a valid observation.

And lo! Thinking, suddenly took a giant leap. The limited thinking of the animals was upgraded to a sophisticated thought-factory.

"Wow – how cool is all this?" the first Human thought looking out from his cave. The progression of Humans speeded up. They started wearing clothes and talking. They discovered fire, invented the wheel, began painting on the cave walls, domesticated animals and started growing food. The learnings had accelerated.

"How did all this speed up?", you may ask.

It is because of the thought-factory. It has enabled faster learning. Much more rapidly than what could be learned through primitive thoughts and information encoded in the body and passed through generations.

The Humans had evolved at a blazingly fast speed, and for a brief period, everyone looked jubilant and peaceful. Then the trouble started.

The thin haze of thoughts churned out by the thought-factory took the form of a dense fog, which made it difficult to see clearly, though. People were stealing, bullying, sulking in despair and fuming with jealousy.

"Why?" you ask in a concerned tone.

The thoughts that helped them learn things had now gone out of control as the thought-factory in their minds churned out one thought after another. Most of these appeared mysteriously without any apparent source or logic, and most of these thoughts made them feel and do uncool things.

They now had a box of dense thoughts around them. They could no longer focus, nor see what was really going on.

———⊱✿⊰———

"So how do we fix this?" you ask, dejected.

"Don't worry", I try to cheer you up, "The *way we think* is evolving towards it fullest potential. And all this trouble is just a temporary side effect of that evolution."

"What do you mean by *'way we think'*?" you ask raising your eyebrows.

"The w*ay we think* or *thinking* is the way we engage with *thoughts* through our *attention.* And just like our senses have evolved over ages –*thinking* is also a sense that is evolving"

"And what will it evolve to?" you seem encouraged. I pause for a moment as you focus your attention in anticipation of this very crucial piece of revelation.

"Putting it simply, in its evolved form, we will be able to *think when we want to and not think when we do not want to*"

"Is that *it*?" you mumble after a pause, *"Think when I want to and not think when I do not want to? "*, you have a skeptical look on your face," that seems like a very simple thing ..."

"It is indeed", I smile, "but isn't it surprising that most of the humanity is unable to do this simple thing?" I pause, " Can you?"

"How long will it take? ", you reply after a long pause," to evolve the way I think?"

'*It can happen right now*", I smile, "If you know the right trick, you can evolve the way you think at this very moment. But for most of us, it will take some time to *understand* the trick in its true sense"

"What do I need to do to understand the trick?"

"You will first need to understand what thoughts are made of. You will then need to explore what attention really is. Then you will finally need to make the effort to understand the interplay between attention and thoughts", I pause.

"And you will need to explore all this *experientially* and not through concepts and theories," I look deep into your eyes, trying to gauge your resolve.

"When do I start?" you smile.

THINKING & THOUGHTS

If you know the right trick, you can evolve the way you think at this very moment.

I am sure that we have all experienced in one way or other, the seemingly innocuous event of our attention being hijacked by a thought. Therefore we should be able to easily *see* the fact that our attention (or the entity that gets hijacked) is different and distinct from *thoughts* (the hijacker).

From this we should be able to logically and experientially relate to the fact that the interplay between thoughts and our attention is what we know as *thinking*.

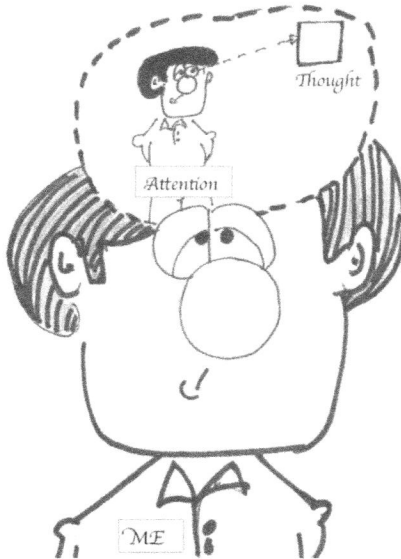

Let us now visualize each of these thoughts as a card with some information encoded within it. A stream of these cards line up – one at a time – to attract my attention. We will use this metaphor of 'person in my head' to represent attention as we explore the various interplays of our mind.

Bad & Good Thinking

My attention starts moving through this stream of cards that we perceive as fleeting images and head talk. These nontangible but powerful cues that we recognize as thoughts then line up in a sequence - conjuring fascinating stories and narratives. These narratives are then spiced up by our neurobiology with emotions and feelings making our attention a captive audience of this show.

This type of interplay between our thoughts and attention is also known as mental chatter. We will refer to this, mainly to emphasize the amount of trouble it can cause, as *bad thinking*. This is first of two main types of thinking.

Recent studies in neuroscience have identified a specific network in our brain called *Default Mode Network* or DMN, which is activated during this chatter. This network becomes active when we are not engaged in focused problem solving. It has been found out in these studies that certain skill can be used to shut down the activity of this network voluntarily thereby shutting down the mental chatter.

This is the same skill that we are going to explore and learn in this book.

The second type of thinking is related to focused problem solving. This type of thinking is usually productive and forms the basis of most of the social and scientific progress that we see around us. This type of thinking is why thinking and thoughts are commonly considered as a virtuous gift. We will refer to this type of thinking as *good thinking*. In this type of thinking, we are able to focus our attention to *create* a sequence of thoughts to solve a problem.

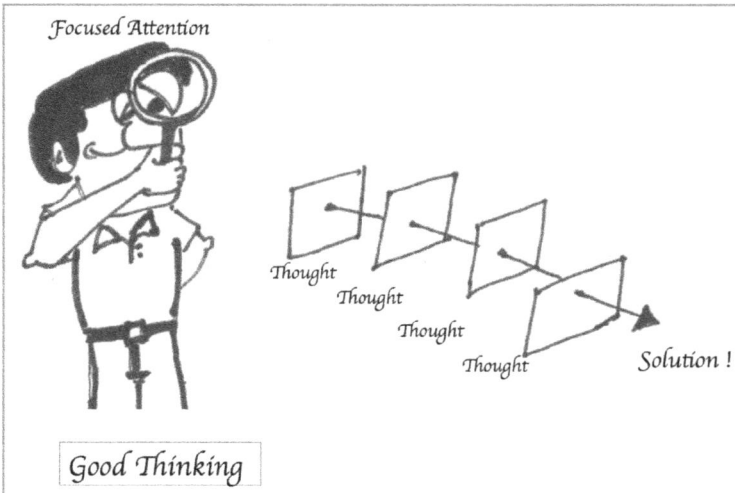

In neuroscience, the Task Positive Network or the TPN is attributed to this type of focused thinking.

Default Mode Network

The default mode network (DMN), also known as default network, or default state network, is a network of eleven interacting brain regions whose activity is highly correlated with each other.

This Network activates by default when a person is **not** Involved in a goal-oriented task. It is active when one is having non-directional thoughts that can be characterized as mental chatter. It has also been shown via scientific studies that shutting down of the DMN reduces random mental chatter.

Task Positive Network

This is a network of interacting brain regions that become active during attention demanding tasks. This network is inversely correlated with the Default Mode Network, which basically means that activity in this part of the brain is affected when the DMN becomes active. Or in other words the brain activity during attention demanding tasks shuts down when mental chatter becomes active.

We all know experientially that we are not able to perform attention-demanding tasks in presence of mental chatter. This fact has now been proven scientifically.

A large majority of the activities that we perform at school or at work involve focused attention. If we could somehow *reduce the DMN activity*, wouldn't it *enhance our ability to effectively perform* these activities that need focused attention?

The answer is an obvious yes. But how do we shut down the DMN?

It has been shown through recent studies that meditators have been able to *voluntarily* shut down the Default Mode Network. And the skills that meditators engage to turn down this mental chatter is the *same skill we intend to develop through the teachings and exercises in this book*.

Thought & Emotions

Our thoughts make us feel the way we do. This fact is a critical link of the trick that we are going to learn to get out of the grip of our mental chatter.

Thoughts cause neurochemical changes in our body. This happens mainly through neuropeptides that are released through our brain into our bloodstream and then eventually expresses itself in form of emotions in our body.

Thoughts and the emotion they invoke are closely related. These emotions or feelings express themselves through a specific pattern of sensations in our body. These sensations can be pleasant or unpleasant and are the final expression of all our emotions.

Cue-thoughts & Action-thoughts

Thought is the key player in any mode of thinking that we engage in - good or bad. If we dive deeper, we will be able to notice that the there are two distinct types of thoughts that drive these two modes of thinking.

The first of these two types, we will refer to as *Cue-thought*. These are the type of thoughts that drive our mental chatter. A cue-thought has two main components: first is an image (or alternatively mental talk) and second is a feeling. These cues can be positive or negative and once these cues are able to grab our attention, they set the course of our thinking.

These cue-thoughts are created from our past experiences and are a convenient evolutionary trick for keeping us alive by aligning our current responses with our past good or bad experiences. We will dive deeper into this topic later in the book where we will explore why these thoughts that kept us safe in the past, are mostly irrelevant today and have unknowingly become the root cause of most of the problems in our life.

The second type of thought called *Action-thought* involves images and mental talk required for problem solving. Unlike cue-thought, it does not have a feeling component.   This type of thought guides and formulates a structured response to a problem. It is this second type of thought that is commonly recognized as *thinking* and is universally considered as a positive trait.

Verbal intonation is an important part of action-thought where words are used to structure the task or actions. These words can then be used as an internal cue or to communicate with others. Another key part is the compilation of *classification* that we have built up over time that helps us classify the apples and the oranges. *Sequencing of actions* is yet another key mechanism. Action-thoughts could be trained to incorporate what we know as *skills*.

Just like a clever advertisement, the fleeting impression of a cue-thought baits our attention interrupting the current track of thinking. When this occurs, our thinking can end up taking a totally unpredictable pathway.

In the most evolved interplay between thoughts & attention, *thoughts no longer distract our attention*. In this interplay we can think when we want to and no think when we do not want to. This advanced interplay is *mindful thinking* and we are going to learn the trick how to perform it in this book. In this advanced interplay, we *do not stop thinking.* It is just that our attention gets trained to resist the lure of mental chatter.

In order to get there, we will need to start by understanding the most common interplay between thoughts and our attention. In this interplay, attention is more or less held captive by cue-thoughts.

Jumping from one cue to other, often without even realizing this fact, our attention stays fragmented and distracted. This distraction has grown considerably in the digital age where these cues get triggered by an incessant stream of information our senses now have access to. These cue-thoughts make our attention distracted and fragmented which expresses itself via inefficiency and mistakes.

Our attention can go beyond fragmentation to a state of stupor, identifying itself totally with the thoughts. The cue-thoughts now act almost like a metaphorical box that blinds our attention. We can visualize this box to be made of interlocking pieces – each one a unique cue-thought that is linked to another.

Understanding this Box is key to understanding the trick to free us from the grip of uncontrolled thoughts.

THE BOX

Thought

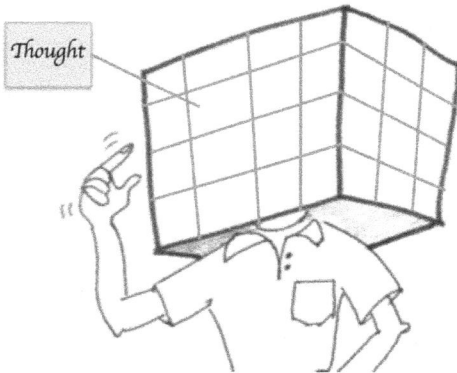

T his box of thoughts shapes the way we see things and eventually our actions. It not only makes us miss out seeing things that are there, it also makes us see things that are not there. It is like seeing things through fogged glasses.

Based on the extent this box obstructs our attention, we can be one of *Boxed, Semi-Unboxed* or *Unboxed.*

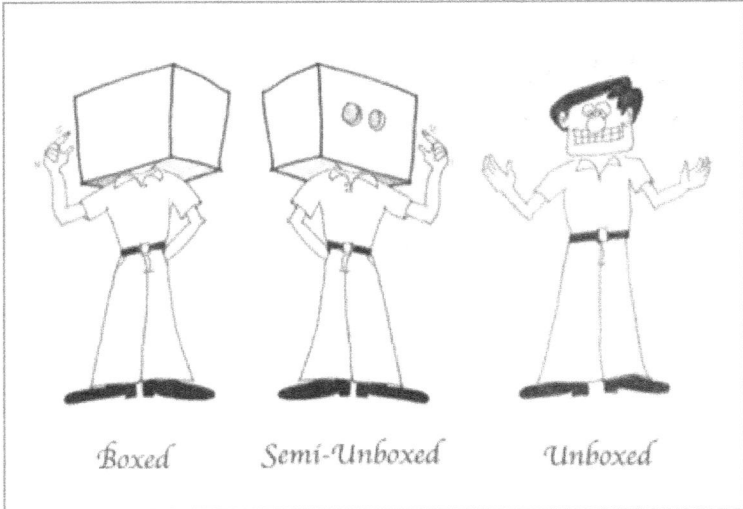

Boxed   Semi-Unboxed   Unboxed

The *Boxed* are those whose attention is captivated by cue-thoughts that are based on past experiences.

There is parable from the east about "The Blind Men and the Elephant" that was made famous in the west by American Poet John Godfrey Saxe. Here is an adapted composition to explain the *Boxed.*

THE BOXED MEN AND THE OX.

There were three Boxed men from Willcox
To learning much inclined,
Who went to see an Ox
That each by observation
Might satisfy his mind.

The First approached the Ox,
And happening to fall
Against his broad and sturdy side,
At once began to bawl:
"God bless me!
But the Ox is like a wall!"

The Second, feeling the horns,
Tried to rein his fear:
"So very round and smooth and sharp?
To me 'tis mighty clear
This wonder of an Ox
Is very like a spear!"

The third no sooner had begun
To feel, the beast, he made no mistake
In, seizing on the swinging tail
That felt real and not at all fake!
"I see," quoth he,
"The Ox is like a snake!"

And so these men from Willcox
Disputed loud and long,
Each in his own opinion
Exceeding stiff and strong,
Though each was partly in the right,
And all were in the wrong!

Through our boxes, we have an obscured view of the world that comes filtered through the lens of our knowledge and experiences. Contrary to what a Boxed person believes, none of these experiences or knowledge can act as an alternative to the ability to see without the obstruction of the box.

Let is see what happens if we somehow punch eyeholes through the box opening up a limited space through which we can now see without the obstruction of cue-thoughts.

Even as the eyeholes appear,
The partially right speculations and fight
Over the wall, rope and the spear
Vanish when they see what is right,
The thing that is actually here!

The *Semi-Unboxed* person from Willcox was able to see the whole Ox. This restricted view through the eyehole made all the difference to appreciate the object for what it is - but not its relation to the larger canvas that exists around it.

The semi-unboxed have a reasonably balanced and mature perspective. These semi-unboxed folks have the potential of becoming completely unboxed. Unfortunately they also hold the possibility to regress into the boxed way of thinking.

And what happens when the entire box is taken off? We can see even better. We now have an unobstructed view of what is really going on, with all the color and shades.

The unboxed thinkers are the rare people who can see beyond the haze of thoughts. They can use thoughts as a tool and not get controlled by them. Their actions are not impacted by greed or fear but rather stems from creativity and reflects what truly needs to be done in a given situation. These are the folks who are true leaders - mostly smiling, calm and unaffected by even the most unwanted situations. They are happy and help others to discover happiness. Today, more than ever, the world needs more unboxed thinkers.

If sufficient numbers of unboxed thinkers assume leadership positions in economic, political and social organizations, this world will be transformed into a different place.

Getting around the Box

A large number of people pretend that the box does not exist. They go through their life falling and hurting themselves, puzzled and worried – but never suspecting that their head was stuck inside a box.

Thankfully an equally significant number of people have sensed the presence of the box and have been looking for ways to get around it.

Many great thinkers have thought about the box from within the box of their own thoughts. They have thought hard about questions like *who made the box* and where *was the box made?*

Many of the answers these boxed thinkers could come up with were at best small parts of the entire puzzle. On their own, they *seemed* correct but each answer was different from the other. Just like the men from Willcox, these thinkers were making the mistake of speculating about the box from the confines of their own.

> *Though each was partly in the right,*
> *and all were in the wrong!*

OK! I see where your Box was made in....

It was made in China !

There was one more approach that was popularly followed as a way to get around the Box. At some point, a semi-unboxed or an unboxed person, knowingly or unknowingly, created a list of rules or insights to help the boxed people navigate the world. These practical rules and insights were very appealing to the boxed folks.

These boxed folks, like our friends from Willcox, were tired of being gored by the Ox despite making logically flawless speculations about walls, spears, snakes and such. They were therefore thrilled to receive guidance on how to behave in the presence of an Ox that they could not see from a person who purportedly could see one.

But there was a problem. Though this guidance worked well in specific scenarios as navigational help, they became ineffective when the maps changed. Let's explore this a bit more using our metaphorical residents of Willcox.

Guidance on how to behave in presence of an Ox was formulated by an unboxed thinker who could see the Ox. This included a list of do's and don'ts for blind boxed folks to help them deal with the animal.

Instructions to keep you safe from an Ox

Ox is an animal that you cannot see. It is big and can be dangerous when provoked. These rules can keep you safe from the Ox:

Rule 1: If something that you touch feels like a snake – it may be Ox's tail. Let it go!

Rule 2: If something that you touch feels like a spear, it may be Ox's horns. Stay away from it!

Rule 3: If something that you touch feels like a wall, it may be Ox's side. Walk away!

Then multitude of grateful boxed followers in Wilcox followed these instructions provided by their unboxed master to say safe from the quirky beast.

Thousands of years pass. Wilcox is now an urban jungle devoid of livestock. It now has a rather big problem of a growing population of rats! But the boxed residents still follow the rules passed along the generations. The rules that kept them safe from Ox, unfortunately, were not at all relevant in keeping them safe from the small vermin. The boxed followers keep on becoming more and more agitated and Wilcox's fate hangs on a thread waiting for the next of unboxed thinker to arrive and update the instructions to handle rats.

Take the Box off

I have realized (and I hope that you would concur) that *learning how to take off the box* is a much more reliable approach than remaining boxed and waiting for the next unboxed master to show up with the next set of rules.

Unfortunately, too many of us have never even considered this option because most of us think that the trick to take the box off would need some sort of superhuman skills that only likes of monks or demigods possess. This is not true. The trick is actually so simple that it is almost funny if we do not get it.

So here is the simple method to take the box off. Please pay attention because the simplicity of this approach makes it difficult to understand.

> *We will first cut eyeholes in the box and then take it off completely.*

"This looks frightfully simple" you raise your eyebrows skeptically.

"It does, doesn't it", I smile, "But that is indeed the trick to take the box off."

"And why can't I just yank it right off?" you ask after a pause, "Why not just two steps – Boxed and Unboxed?"

"It is because this box is invisible to you. You do not know where the box is and therefore are unable to take it off."

"Hmmm ... the box that blinds my view is itself imperceptible?" you mumble.

"Yes, you cannot see it or feel it. So you need to perform some tricks and first, make eyeholes appear so that you can detect the box. The box now stands out in contrast to the holes."

"Hmm the eyeholes give away the location of the box?" you squint in concentration. I nod.

"And after that?"

"After that, it is quite simple. Once you can *see* the box - it can be yanked right off. I will now show you how to do that."

MIND-GYM SESSION ONE

E ach Mind-Gym Session, like this one, would come
with a set of *exercises*. The purpose of these
exercises is to make the learnings experiential.

General Instructions

Each exercise is followed by a set of follow-up notes
that dive deeper based on your observations from the
exercises. Please do not read these notes before you
complete the exercise. Also, these exercises and notes
intend to create insights that are from outside the
track of our usual thoughts so we need to resist the
pressure to get the right answer to the raised
questions. We just need to follow the notes with
earnestness.

The Mind-gym sessions also introduce *techniques* to exercise your mind muscles. These techniques can be organized under three categories:

1. Warm-Up: These are preparatory routines that facilitate the core routines or exercises.
2. Core: These are the core techniques that build up the core *mind muscles* to take the box off.
3. Strengthening routines: These are exercises that are done during and around our day-to-day activities. These routines strengthen our core practice and accelerate the process of taking the box off.

The sessions also recommend an assignment that comes with a set of activities, exercises, and schedule. These assignments need to be performed regularly to reap the true benefits of the Mind-Gym.

Basic Prep

Most of these techniques need to be performed while you are sitting erect in a comfortable position. You can either sit on a chair or cross-legged on a mat. Please use a lower back support using a cushion.

Assignments

The practical sessions will end with an assignment that comes with a set of activities, exercises, and a schedule.

With all these tools at your disposal please note that there is no shortcut for the effort that is required to get out of that box. Knowing the concepts theoretically is not going to cut it.

You will need to experientially understand the simple trick to unbox, which is the purpose of all these exercises, routines and assignments.

Exercise 1: Exploring attention

Sit comfortably on a chair in a quiet place.

Extend your palms in front of you, thumbs touching, facing out at the height of your ears.

Part 1: Keep your gaze fixed on the back of your thumbs. Pay full attention to one of the thumbs; notice all details – the texture of the skin, the grooves, the scars, and the color. Do this for at least fifteen seconds. Make a mental note of the 'quality' of this attention.

Part 2: Now take the palms apart and gently back towards your ears, keeping your gaze in front without moving your eyes. Back of the palms will now be

---

'seen' in your peripheral vision. Take the palms as far back as you can – lining them with your ears, while you can still 'see' both of them simultaneously in your peripheral vision.

Now, while maintaining the palms in your vision, be aware of the top of your head and your toes *at the same time*. Hold this for at least fifteen seconds.

Make a mental note of the 'quality' of this *expanded* attention that you have now.

Notes:

- Did your attention wander into thoughts when you were trying to pay attention to the back of your palms in Part1?
- Did you notice the difference in the quality of attention at the end of Part 2 – as compared to the focused attention at the end of Part 1?
- Could you feel thoughts in the state of expanded attention? Usually we experience very little or no thoughts in this state. You can repeat the exercise again to confirm this.

Please get familiar with this 'preview' of expanded attention. Here are the key characteristics of this attention:

1. Thoughts stop or slow down in the initial 10-15 seconds we try to hold this state.
2. You feel more relaxed and *expanded*.
3. You are aware of *everything around you* rather than focusing or concentrating on something in particular.
4. You still retain your ability to respond based on your learnings.
5. If you try out this exercise for a longer duration, you will notice an increased ability to 'watch' the thoughts rising in your mind.

This transient state that you experienced is an approximation of how unboxed thinkers perceive the world. Through the course of this book we will learn to make this mode of thinking lasting and deep.

Exercise 2: Exploring thoughts
You will need: A notebook, a pencil.

Close your eyes for two minutes and put your attention on your thoughts.

Note down the number of thoughts you can recall.

What was the form of the thoughts? Did you see a visual – an image? What else? Maybe sounds? Voice?

Close your eyes again for a minute. Pay attention to the visual part of the thought. It can be very fleeting and faint. Almost like a 'pre-image,' where a faint impression flashes to give an idea of the picture. This faint impression can also have an audio track of head talk. Can you *see* all of this?

Were these images from past? Future? Were there any random visuals that you cannot place? What was the craziest image?

Your mind may try to skip answering these questions. Please hold the determination to answer these honestly to yourself.

Notes:

- Did you notice that the visual or 'image' is an essential part of thoughts?
- Did you notice the quantity of thoughts bubbling through the mind? There is almost one every second on an average but we are not aware of most of them.
- Did you also notice that these thoughts could be random and nowhere related to what you are doing right now?

Exercise 3: Exploring the nature of recall
You will need: A phone or computer with internet access.

Watch a 30-second video clip of your choice that has *very little motion in it*. A close-up of one of your favorite singers may work well.

You can also try watching the first 30 seconds of the extended trailer of Planet Earth II. The trailer is on YouTube and the initial minute or so has slow moving images.

Now close your eyes and recall what you saw.

Notes:

- Could you remember the video exactly? In High Definition - comparable to what you watched?

- Most of us may be able to recall the video clip and recreate a significant part if it in our mind.

Exercise 4: Exploring the nature of recall once more
You will need: A phone or computer with Internet access.

Now watch another 10-second video. This one should have a lot of movements – like in a dance sequence.

You can also try watching the last 30 seconds of the extended trailer of Planet Earth II.

Close your eyes and recall what you saw.

Notes:

- Could you recall the clip exactly?

- Can you "see" that the recall was a sequence of visuals or *images* and not a continuous video? (You may have to perform this exercise a few times to see this clearly.)
- Did you notice that our mind serves us a sequence of static visuals or images and makes us believe that we are watching the entire video?
- Can you *see* that the recalled thought is more like a cleverly edited 'trailer' of the original clip that gives the gist – but is in no way the real thing?
- Can you now repeat Exercise 2 (slow moving video) and notice that even there we recalled a sequence of static images? It was hard to detect this fact because the images did not change so much across frames.
- How is this recall different from the recall of a concept or a formula?

Exercise 5: Exploring the nature of recall one last time

Observe an activity going around you for 30 seconds or so with full attention. Make sure this activity has some known people involved.

Close your eyes and try to recall exactly what you just saw.

Notes:

- Can you be attentive enough to notice the approximation of the images in the recall? What does this say about our capacity to recall things accurately?

- How is *this* recall different than the recall of a concept, formula or a tool from a subject that you studied in school or college?

The recall of activities of known people around you will most likely come with a track of emotions (mostly influenced by persons you are observing) in addition to the images. This emotion track will be missing during recall of concept, formula or a tool. Can you try to see this and try to find out why is this so?

Our thoughts are based on our past. They are influenced by past events or projection of past events into the future. So our thoughts are in someway tapping into our ability to recall. This recall is in turn dependent in the way we had recorded the past experience.

These experiences were recorded with a track of emotions experienced at the time. These recordings eventually influence our cue-thoughts.

> *Our recall is imperfect. It is at best a close approximation of what actually happened. Our thoughts depend on this recall and therefore are also imperfect.*

Recording of concepts, skills or tools usually come without the track of emotions. These recordings influence our action-thoughts.

Examining the nature of our recall and its limitations can help us understand the limitation of thoughts that depend on this recall.

Mind-Gym Technique 1: Belly Breathing.
Category: Strengthening routine

Belly breathing is the natural form of breathing that increases our capacity not to get distracted by thoughts.

With longer practice, it may also reduce the number of thoughts generated in our mind.

The technique is quite simple. Make sure your belly goes up when you breathe in, and it goes in when you breathe out.

This type of breathing is different from chest breathing where the chest goes out (and belly goes in) when we breathe in, and the chest goes in (and belly out) when we breathe out.

Exercise 6: Effects of Belly Breathing.
You will need: A timer with alarm, a notebook, and a pencil.

Sit comfortably on a mat or on a chair. Focus on the belly as you breathe.

Breathe in – Belly out. Breathe out – Belly in.

Do this for five minutes with your eyes closed. You should use a timer to keep track of time.

Close eyes and watch thoughts for two more minutes. Try to pay attention to the visuals or images.

How many number of visual or images can you recall? Note down the number.

Notes:

- Were the thoughts lesser than what you noticed in Exercise 2?
- Are you feeling more relaxed?

Belly breathing helps calm down the flow of thoughts. It is the natural way to breathe Most of the small kids belly-breathe naturally.

Exercise 7: Effect of habitual (chest) breathing
You will need: A timer with alarm, a notebook, and a pencil.

Sit comfortably on a mat or on a chair. Close your eyes and perform *chest breathing* for two minutes.

The chest goes out (and belly goes in) when we breathe in, and the chest goes in (and belly out) when we breathe out. Close eyes and watch thoughts for two minutes. Try to pay attention to the images.

How many can you recall? Note down the number.

Notes:

- Chest breathing helps in situations where we need more oxygen than normal – which is usually during physical strain.
- Chest breathing makes us more wired up. Do you feel this after the exercise? Did you notice that the number of thoughts went up as compared to belly breathing?

Most of us perform habitual chest breathing even when we are not in physically demanding situations. This makes us wired up, and increases the number of thoughts in mind.

Exercise 8: Nature of thoughts
You will need: A timer with alarm.

Sit comfortably on a mat or on a chair.

> Close eyes and think about an amusing incident from your life. An event that makes you happy. Take two minutes to do this.

Notes:

- Did you notice the image or images in your thoughts? Did they make you happy?
- Where did you 'feel' happiness?
- What was the exact sensation of being happy: blushing face, tingling stomach etc.? Did you feel something in the head, around the ears?
- Can you *see* the link between the feeling of happiness and the sensation it creates?

Assignment:

Day						
✔ 1	✔ 2	3	4	5	6	7
8	9	10	11	12	13	14
15	16	17	18	19	20	21
22	23	24	25	26	27	28

- Try to do as much belly breathing as possible. Preferably through all your daily activities except when you are exercising, playing or doing strenuous chores.

Connecting the Dots

- Thinking is the way we engage with thoughts through our attention. This 'way we think' has evolved over the ages and is still evolving.

- There are two types of thoughts: cue-thoughts and action thoughts. These influence two modes of thinking: Bad Thinking, and Good Thinking.

- Mental chatter acts like a box through which our attention cannot see clearly. The trick to free our attention from this chatter is to take off this metaphorical box.

- We can take this Box off through two steps:

    1. The first step is to 'see' that the box exists and stands out in contrast to eyeholes in it. We call this state as 'Semi Unboxed.'

    2. Once the box is seen, it can be yanked right off to get the 'Unboxed' state.

- The trick to take the box is very simple and can help you take it off *right now*. But usually it takes some time to understand the trick in its true sense.

- In order to help us understand the trick we start by experientially exploring our attention, our ability to recall and our thoughts.

GOOD THINKING

> *Good thinking is a harmonized play between our attention and thoughts.*

You are trying to solve an important problem. Your thinking is focused and you use all the tools and tricks you have learned over the years. For some moments you do not even think. And hey presto, you have a solution!

So what goes on during this type of 'good' thinking?

Let's dive into our mind and find out more. As we pick up a magnifying glass and start our investigation, please take a small pause and pay attention. Attention is an essential part of this *inner stuff*, and we will start by paying attention to attention itself.

Attention

Attention has a significant role to play in the trick we are going to learn. Attention, like a spotlight, shines on things you are aware of. Anything that you feel with your senses or anything that raises in your mind.

It is almost like an invisible *you* at the center of your existence. This does not need any theories, concepts or speculations – your attention defines what you are experiencing *right now*.

Your attention spans the outer world as well as the inner world and defines your zone of awareness. Is your attention on the words of this book? Was that a notification on your smartphone? Did your attention wander momentarily to verify if you heard the sound? Did it shift to thinking about something you are going to do later in the day? Our attention gets easily distracted and more often than not, this distraction comes from the inner world.

We will learn more about these distractions and how to prevent them from fragmenting our attention. This unfragmented attention holds the key to mindful thinking. An unfragmented attention is different from conventional 'focus' and 'concentration.' This expanded flowing awareness enables a new kind of focus that allows you to perform work of your choice without getting distracted. You should have experienced a glimpse of this in MindGym Session One, *Exercise 1: Exploring attention.* It will be a good idea to repeat the exercise once more to make the learning about *attention* more experiential.

So what are these distractions from the inner world that makes our attention selective and shifty? Let's start with the main reason – our thoughts.

Thoughts

If we dive deeper into our mind and observe the thoughts that arise there, we will find two *main* types of thoughts: Action-thoughts, and Cue-thoughts that have been already introduced you to.

"Two *main* types of thoughts? ", you ask, "so are there more?"

There is *one* more.

"That is not fair", you protest? "All this while we have been talking about *two* type of thoughts and now you say there is one more!"

"We will introduce new concepts only when you are ready to experientially verify them", I explain politely, "And we may not yet be ready for the I-Thought."

This third type of thought holds the key to why cue-thoughts end up causing so much trouble. We will, of course explore it in detail later in the book. For now, let's focus on action-thought and cue-thought.

Action-thought, guides and formulates a structured response to a problem. They can be trained to incorporate what we know as *skills*.

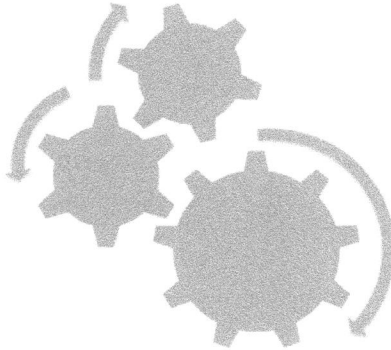

We have, as a society, invested heavily in making our action-thought toolkits more and more efficient. We have continuously devised new and improved skills to help us weave more efficient action-thought stories. These stories then enable more efficient ways to solve a problem.

Cue-thought is a cleverly encoded cue card. Our sensory inputs - seeing, hearing, smelling, tasting and touching, automatically trigger this cue. Most of the time this cue is served without us being aware of it.

If you observe closely, you will be able to see that cue-thought has two key components:

First is visual, a picture or an image. This can also be accompanied by a mental talk. Second is an emotion or feeling, which expresses itself as a bundle of sensations through the body. The emotion can be faint or strong and varies from one cue-thought to the other.

The cue-thought in one way is a kind of an enhanced emoticon – a blend of an image and an emotion. Both the components of the cue-thought 'appear' *almost* at the same time. The emotion appears a fraction of a moment after the image.

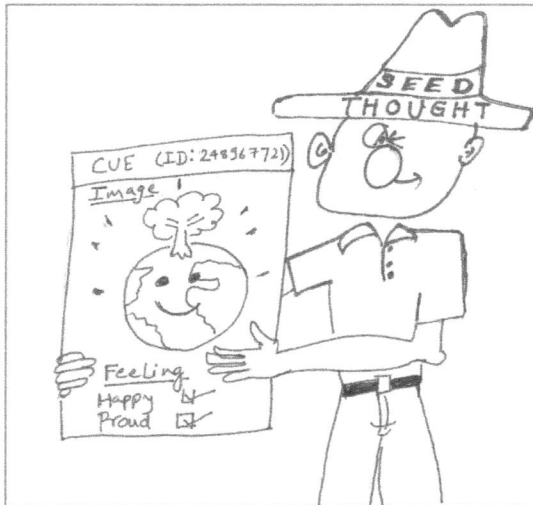

The emotion appears in the body as the image flashes in mind. The image part of the cue-thought is perceived as a visual. This image can also be accompanied by a voice track or *mental talk*. The emotion part of the thought is perceived through sensations. The sensations can be pleasant or unpleasant and appear in a pattern that we can recognize as a 'feeling.'

There can be several kinds of cues, but let us consider the two most important ones. First kind of cue tries to drive actions through Positive reinforcement.

"Psst ... notice the visual that I am showing in the cue. See that? Good. That thing will make you feel this way..." Your attention quickly scans the visual and then moves on to the positive feeling that is part of the cue. The feeling expresses itself as a bundle of sensations in your body, captivating you.

Is it an image of a green earth full of lush green trees? The thought also causes a small 'sample' of happy and proud sensations to arise in your body – almost as bait to reinforce the message it wants to convey.

This trick is very similar to how your attention gets trapped by advertisements in the real world. The cue-thought is the mother of all ads - one that plays within your mind incessantly.

And just like a cleverly crafted advertisement, cue-thought has hooks to grab your attention. Each cue with a different set of visual and a feeling or sensation. In case of positive reinforcement, these feelings and images are of something that you like.

And similar to real world advertisements, the cue-thought could also use negative reinforcement as bait to grab your attention.

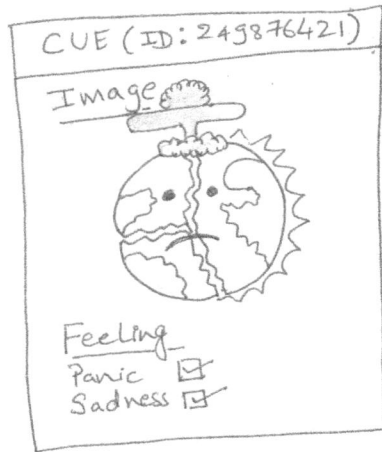

An image of destruction that may get unleashed on the earth? Feelings panic and sadness supplement the visual, embedded within the cue. The visual in this case is an apocalyptic image with nuclear wars and mushroom clouds.

Similar to the real world negative advertisements, negative cues are far more effective in getting a response because negative feelings usually draw our attention more effectively than positive feelings.

Once these positive or negative cues are able to grab our attention with sufficient intensity, they set our course of action based on the message the cue just conveyed to us.

Thinking

In an ideal situation, you attention is able to freely sift trough and engage the best tools and techniques you have learnt to *generate* a sequence of action-thoughts using verbal intonations, a sequence of actions.

This is what we call *good thinking*. This thinking is an effective play between our attention and thoughts. Intention is set by organized action-thoughts and our attention follows these thoughts to fruitful completion.

But some things prevent us from doing this kind of good thinking. Even as we are engaging with the action thoughts with focused attention, suddenly a cue-thought trigger arrives and derails our chain of thoughts.

BAD THINKING

An innocuous and seemingly random cue-thought can change your intention and hi-jack the course of action set by even the most brilliant action-thoughts.

So you start with a great intention of doing something fantastic. You also have all the tools to help you do this great thing. But then as you were doing what you were supposed to do – Bang! You are hit with a random cue-thought that then takes you on a new path and down an unknown rabbit hole of thoughts with a modified intention. This intention is not that great.

Have you ever wondered why are you watching YouTube videos or playing a game in the middle of preparing for an office assignment or a test? Or why do you think about your last vacation in the midst of a meeting? Or perhaps about a meeting in the midst of your vacation? It is because of a cue-thought that hijacked your attention.

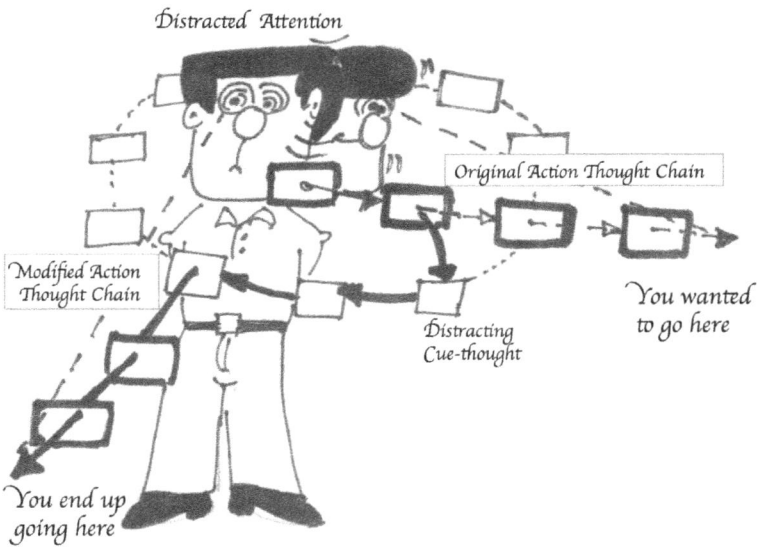

You are mostly in charge when you are creating action-thoughts. *But you are NOT in charge of the cue-thoughts that get triggered in a given situation and change your intention altogether.*

These cue-thoughts appear automatically - triggered by your current situation. There are an enormous number of these cue-thoughts that are just waiting to spring up and capture your attention. These cue-thoughts play a vital role in luring the mind into creating irrelevant thought stories. And when this happens – it is 'Bad' thinking.

These random cue-thoughts make our attention restless and eventually, our attention can become dazed and completely captivated by them.

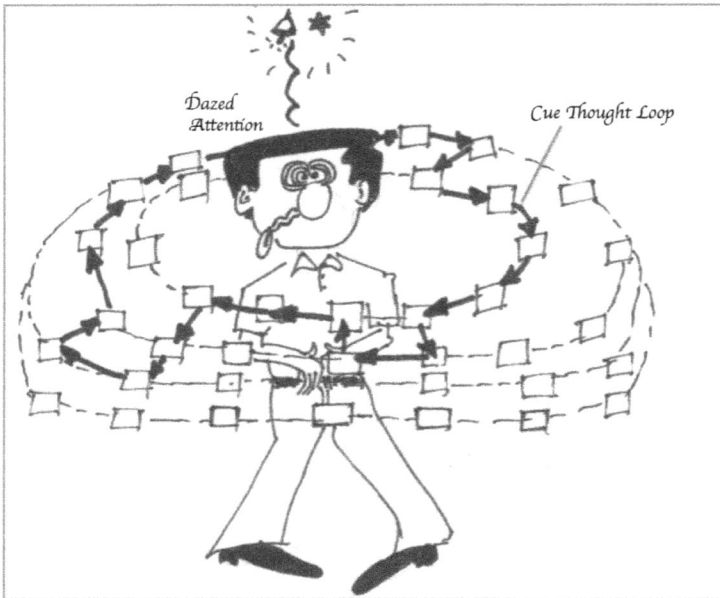

Once our attention is captivated, these cue-thoughts drive your life, hindering you from using action-thoughts at will. You can no longer *think when you want to and not think when you do not want to.*

'That sounds awful!" I hear you say as your deepest fears are confirmed, "How can I stop these cue-thoughts?"

"We can't really stop them", I reply, "but that does not mean that we cannot do anything about them."

We can train our attention *not to grab onto* these cue-thoughts. This simple approach is the core of all effective mindfulness techniques across the ages. This training is all we need to Unbox.

Now that we know what are we trying to do – let's dive into how to do it.

MIND-GYM SESSION TWO

———— ❦ ————

In the last session, we saw that an 'image' was part of our thoughts. We also saw that breathing could be used to calm down thoughts. Now we explore another important aspect of thoughts: Emotions or feelings and the sensations they create in our body.

Exercise 1: Watching sensations
You will need: A scary move clip, a timer, a pencil and a notebook.

Watch a scary clip from any movie of your choice for five minutes.

Did you feel scared? If not watch some more until you are!

Close eyes and feel the sensations in your body. Take notice of the sensations you are feeling:

Make a not of the applicable sensations out of this list:

- Churning in the stomach

- Tingling in the face

- Tingling in the back and spine

- Flushing of face

- Contraction in face, chest or abdomen

- Heaviness in head, chest or abdomen

Notes:

- Can you identify the unique 'pattern' of sensations that can be linked to the feeling of being scared?

Mind-Gym Technique2: Watching Sensations
Category: Core

A big part of being aware of the Cue-thoughts is building the ability to 'sense' the sensations associated with the feelings part of these cues. Using this technique, we will enhance our capacity to be aware of such sensations.

Sit comfortably on a mat or on a chair with your back erect.

Start belly breathing. After five minutes, move your attention to your entire abdomen area. Your focus will no longer be your breath, which can now be whatever is natural.

Scan your abdomen slowly, being aware of all sensations on the skin. You may observe tickling, throbbing, buzzing or pricking sensations. Do not try to analyze these sensations in any way – just watch. Don't label them as good or bad. Don't try to think why a specific sensation is happening in a particular way.

Move up to your chest area. Then to your face, spending at least two minutes in each zone.

Now move down from the rear of your head to neck, then upper back and then lower back, spending two minutes in each area. The whole exercise will take 10-12 minutes.

Notes:

- Most of the sensations caused by our feelings have a pattern that appears in the space that we just scanned. With practice, we will be able to spot these sensations and 'diffuse' them before these feelings erupt into thought stories.

- Try to pay attention to any 'discomfort" you feel through your day. Approach this discomfort with a sense of curiosity to observe its patterns. This ability will you help immensely.
- Repeat Exercise 1. This time watch the sensations using Mind-Gym technique2.
- Did the feeling of fear fade away as you watched its sensations?
- Did the feeling of fear change to something else while you 'watched' it?
- What sensation did it transform into?

Assignment

Day						
1	2	3 ✔	4 ✔	5	6	7
8	9	10	11	12	13	14
15	16	17	18	19	20	21
22	23	24	25	26	27	28

1. Observe the sensations that are created in your body after watching an engrossing advertisement on TV.
2. Observe the sensations that are created in your body after watching a news clip on TV. Can these sensations be possibly linked to cue-thoughts these programs might be triggering?

3. Strengthening routine
- Try to do as much belly breathing as you can.

4. Core
- Observe your body sensations (Technique 2) before you go to sleep.

Connecting the Dots

- There are two distinct parts of the brain correlated with two different types of thinking: mental chatter and focused problem solving.
- Default Mode Network or DMN becomes active where there is mental chatter. The Task Positive Network or TPN is correlated to focused problem solving.
- Thoughts produce emotions via neurochemicals released by our brain. These emotions appear as a distinct pattern of sensations in our body.
- Cue-thoughts are related to mental chatter and action-thoughts to focused problem solving.
- Cue-thought is like 'cue' or advertisement that attracts our attention and influences it to follow a modified course of action. This type of thinking is what we call *Bad Thinking*.
- A cue-thought has two components that it uses to capture our attention: (1) An image or mental talk & (2) An emotion.

- Action thoughts utilize the tools and techniques that we learn in our life. *Good Thinking* is interplay between action-thoughts and our attention.
- Cue-thoughts can transform good thinking into bad thinking.
- *Mindful Thinking* helps us to do less of bad thinking and more of good thinking. We do so by training our attention not to engage with cue-thoughts.
- We explored the impact of thoughts on our emotions and also examined the pattern of sensations that are caused by emotions.
- We learned the technique of *watching* sensations in order to develop the skill to be able to 'spot' the sensation part of cue-thoughts. This skill, as we will see later, will help us to 'let-go' of cue-thoughts.

LESS OF BAD THINKING

———— ❧ ————

> *Bad Thinking happens when cue-thoughts hijack our attention.*

What exactly are these cue-thoughts? And how do they throw us off from our intended actions?

Each cue-thought is a condensed nugget from a distinct experience. These nuggets are stored in our mind and get triggered when our body-mind senses a situation similar to that in the past. This trigger happens automatically without coming into our attention. Just like the beating of our heart and digestion of our food, we don't have control on this trigger.

In situations where there are multiple matches from the past, multiple cue-thoughts are triggered in succession. A multitude of these thoughts get triggered over the course of the day, sometimes several every moment. Some of us can consciously notice these cues but most cannot.

We have already observed that cue-thought has two components bundled into it: One is a picture or image. Other is a feeling or a bundle of sensations through the body. Both of these appear almost at the same time. The feeling appears in the body as the image flashes in mind. This feeling is defined by a bundle of sensations that appear in our body.

From a simple feeling of liking or disliking – to more complex ones like fear, desire, aversion or hatred, each has it's own pattern of sensations: throbbing, flushing, aching, radiating, comforting, tingling, tickling spread across the body.

This, in fact, was a very clever feature devised by nature to ensure a quick response based on past experiences. This 'feature' worked very well when we lived in primitive and unsafe settings that were riddled with danger.

Way back in the past, when we were still living in forests infested by poisonous snakes, I witnessed the sad outcome of snakebite due to which I lost a companion. I unknowingly created a powerful cue-thought at that time. This cue-thought had an image of a snake and a feeling of terror. This freshly minted cue-thought was added to a small list of similar other cue-thoughts, mostly around the situations I could die: Lion, terror; Tiger, terror; Fire, terror – you get the idea. Primitive cue-thoughts were structured mostly around the feeling of fear.

So, next time I saw something slithering, this very powerful cue-thought with the image of a snake and feeling of terror was served to me. This cue hijacked the control of my mind from whatever I was doing and created a fresh set action-thoughts *"Run as fast as you can."* And thus this cue-thought helped me stay alive. Mother nature overrode whatever intention I had in my mind with a new intention: *stay alive.*

There was a small side effect of this otherwise perfect tool. The cue-thought got triggered even when I saw something that remotely resembled a snake. A vine, a dried twig, or a rope. As a result, I stopped doing whatever I was doing and ran as fast I could every time this happened. I was terrified each of these times – but I could not complain because the damn cue-thought kept me safe from snakes.

Then one day I moved out of the forest to a land where there were no snakes. I still kept jumping and running as fast as I could whenever I saw a vine, a dried twig or a rope. And this was not the only cue-thought that remained stored within me. I had a huge big collection of them that kept me jumping in panic around every corner.

There was another peculiar thing about these cue-thoughts - they had a way of getting passed down over generations. This was why everyone had such a big collection of them. Though most of these thought triggers had become redundant over time, they remained in our minds - as effective in commanding our attention as they were when they got created.

These ancient cues point to a set of actions that are also very primitive. As attention latches onto a cue, captivating stories from the past and projections into the future are spun out.

We may not have control of how these cues are triggered but we can do two things to reduce their impact. First and most importantly, we can learn to ignore these cues. This is the main skill we will develop using Mind-Gym techniques.

And once we get a hang of this skill, we will try to make these cues fewer. We will learn how to create fewer of new ones and also how to 'diffuse' some of the more disturbing old cue-thoughts.

Let's now get prepared to exercise our mind-muscles and understand how can we prevent these random cue-thoughts from distracting our attention. Especially the ancient ones that were created thousands of years ago.

MIND-GYM SESSION THREE

In the last session, we had explored the 'feeling' component of cue-thoughts. We also explored how to 'watch' the sensations expressed by a feeling and observed how the sensations faded away or changed when we watched it. This was one of the ways of letting-go of these cue-thoughts. Now we further examine the skill of letting-go of thoughts.

Exercise 1: Watching the distractions
You will need: A smartphone or a laptop with Internet, a pencil and a notebook.

We will now perform a set of exercises involving an activity to deliberately engage your thoughts.

You will need to make a note whenever thoughts distract you. Keep a note of the visual and emotion/feeling associated with these thoughts.

Read chapter one of the classic book "Three men in a boat" written by Jerome K Jerome. The book was written in 1889 and is available in the public domain.

Notes:

- How many times did you wander into thoughts that were not related to the images conveyed by the book?
- For such interruptions, what was the image? What was the emotion?
- Did you drift away into an unusually long thought story?
- Did your drifts impact the overall enjoyment of the reading?

Our breathing plays a very important role in our ability to sense thoughts and feelings. It is the bridge between our body and mind. Have you ever breathed slowly, 'counting to ten' to settle down your anger or anxiety?

We now introduce two Warm-Up techniques that use our breath. These techniques enhance our ability to be aware of our cue-thoughts at the same time *temporarily* reducing the number of thoughts rising in our mind.

Mind-Gym Technique3: Bumble Bee Hum

Category: Warm-Up

Close your eyes.

Place the index and forefinger of each of your hand horizontally over the respective eye. The fingers should exert a gentle pressure on your eyeballs. Now clog each ear with the respective thumb.

Take a deep breath, close your mouth and create a Humming sound "Hummmmm"

Continue until you are out of breath. Feel the vibration in your entire head and face while you Hum.

Repeat this ten times.

Mind-Gym Technique 4: Balanced Breath

Category: Warm-Up

Sit comfortably and erect.

Close eyes and do belly breathing for one minute.

Now close right nostril (with your index finger) and use the left nostril to inhale. When you are ready to exhale, switch the nostril (close left nostril) and exhale completely.

Repeat 20 times.

Exercise 2: Watching the distractions
You will need: A smartphone or a laptop with Internet, a pencil and a notebook.

Read chapter two of "Three men in a boat".

Keep a note whenever thoughts while doing the exercise distract you. Keep a note of the visual and emotion/feeling of these thoughts.

Notes:

- How was the experience this time different from one in Exercise 1? Were there lesser distractions?
- Were you able to come back from the distractions quicker?
- Please try this thought exercise: Imagine that you have developed the ability to ignore cue-thoughts. And you have no work to do and no problems to solve. So you do not have any "action-thoughts" either. What would this "zone" feel like?
- Please revisit the Exercise 1 of Mind-Gym Session One: Exploring Attention.

Assignment

Day						
1	2	3	4	✔ 5	✔ 6	✔ 7
8	9	10	11	12	13	14
15	16	17	18	19	20	21
22	23	24	25	26	27	28

1.Belly breathing (Technique 1): As much as you can through the day.

2. In addition to the above, will now start a **daily Mind-Gym session**. This session can be done at any convenient time but at least two hours after a meal. Please perform these routines indoor in a quiet room, free from interruptions. Sit comfortably on a mat or on a chair with your back erect.

Warm-Up

- 10 times bumblebee Humming (Technique 3)
- 20 times balanced breathing (Technique 4)

Core

- 12 minutes of sensation watching (Technique 2)

MORE OF GOOD THINKING

It is time to learn how to let go of distracting thoughts!

How about we learn how to do this through a simple skit.

"Skit?" you roll your eyes in disbelief, "Why?"

To throw us off our usual train of thoughts and engage us at a deeper level of understanding.

CAST

Ms. Attention: *This person represents your attention.*

Cue-thought: *One cue-thought out of the numerous that control your attention by distracting it. This particular one has been introduced earlier in the book.*

Anchor-thought: *The friendly prop that helps you to get out of the grip of the cue-thought.*

[Stage opens. Ms. Attention is standing on the right side of the stage grabbing the arm of an ancient *Cue-thought* who is dressed like a cave man]

Host [addresses Ms. Attention]: Ms. Attention, aren't you fed-up of being controlled by random thoughts. Especially by one like this [points to the cue-thought who grins, showing a row of blackened teeth].

Ms. Attention: Yes, of course. Please help me! I am caught by this thought. I don't know what to do!

Host [smiles]: I don't want to sound rude, but that thought is not holding you. *You* are holding on to it. Just let go.

Ms. Attention: [in anguish] I cannot!!

Host: You can. Please try it!

[Ms. Attention lets go of the thought momentarily and then holds it back again]

Ms. Attention: I cannot! The cue-thought is capturing me again and again. It is such a bad cue-thought. [Ms. Attention grips the thought more tightly] I cannot leave it!

Host: [Addresses the audience] The situation is serious. She is holding on to the cue-thought but believes that the cue-thought is holding her [The cue-thought gives a sly grin]

Host [to the audience]: I have an idea! I will trick her into leaving that thought.

[Enter, Anchor-thought, who stands on the left side of the stage holding a cardboard anchor]

Host [to Ms. Attention]: You - can you hear me?

[Ms. Attention nods her head]

Reach out and hold *that* thought – standing in that corner [points at Anchor-thought].

[Anchor-thought smiles and points the anchor towards Ms. Attention]

[Ms. Attention leaves the cue-thought, runs across the stage and catches the Anchor-thought's cardboard anchor]

Ms. Attention: That was easy [laughs]. The cue-thought let me go!"

Host: [Host winks at the audience] This trick works because she can hold on to only one thought at a time. Though she has forgotten how to **let go** of thoughts, she is an expert in **grabbing on** to them. See how I have tricked her into letting go of the cue-thought [Points to the cue-thought, who now has a puzzled expression on its face] by having her catch this one [points at anchor-thought, who is smiling].

Host [To Anchor-thought]: Let us make her do this several times until she finds out on her own that the thoughts were not catching her. She was clinging on to the thoughts.

Ms. Attention: [running across the stage and grabbing the cue-thought again]

Well, wait – the bad thought has caught me again!

[Anchor-thought once more points the anchor at Ms. Attention]

Ms. Attention: [running back to the anchor-thought] And now... it has left me again! [This cycle repeats several times after which Ms. Attention stops in the middle of the stage]

Ms. Attention: I see it now! That cue-thought was not catching me. I was clinging on to it. And **I can leave it whenever I want to**!

[The angry cue-thought extends its arms towards Ms. Attention. Ms. Attention runs close to it, barely touching its extended arms and then run back to the center of the stage with a smile on her face]

Ms. Attention: Now I know how to let-go of thoughts! Does that mean I am free from the grip of uncontrolled thoughts?

Host: Yes! Now that you can let-go of this particular distracting thought, you can do it for other cue-thoughts as well. But you will have to keep practicing this trick until till you master it. Then it will be effortless.[Ms. Attention smiles]

Host: [Addresses the audience] Wasn't that simple? Now that you know this trick, **shall we practice it together**?

MIND-GYM SESSION FOUR

I n the last session, we saw how thought-triggers capture our attention. We also saw that breathing exercises reduce these thought triggers to some extent.

Today we will learn the most important technique to build our mind muscles. It is more of a trick than a technique really, because as we saw in the skit, it is our attention that grabs on to the thoughts while it believes that the thoughts have taken it hostage.

We will trick our attention into realizing this (sadly) comical fact.

PLEASE!
Let-go of me!!

Exercise 1: Letting Go

You will need: An apple and an orange (or any two different objects of similar size)

Set the apple and the orange in front of you.

Close your eyes and imagine that you have "forgotten" letting go (of anything you grab). You also have to imagine that you are extremely skillful in grabbing things.

Now gently catch the apple with your right hand. Now pretend that you have forgotten to let go the Apple and are stuck with it.

Now close your eyes and imagine that you are grabbing the orange. You do not need to think anything about letting go of the apple. Just focus on grabbing the orange – you are good at catching after all!

Now gently shift your focus to the orange and grab it with the right hand.

Repeat this several times.

Notes:

- Can you *see* that the action of grabbing the orange automatically forces you to let-go of the Apple?
- Can you relate this with cue-thought and anchor-thought?
- Can you *see* that if you perform structured anchoring (moving to an anchor again and again as explained in the skit), your attention has the opportunity to 'watch' the act of letting-go the cue-thought in each cycle?
- Imagine how would it be to have your Attention at the center of the stage, not getting pulled by any thoughts? How will it feel to be in that zone?

Now it is time to introduce the most important technique in Mind-Gym. The technique is based on the anchor-thought trick that was described in the skit and also in the last exercise. This technique is the core of almost all of the well known and effective mindfulness techniques practiced through ages.

Like all of the Mind-Gym techniques, this one too is rooted in time-tested approaches with a range of traditional names. In our thought-based approach, we have deliberately avoided all such references that can potentially create an unintended bias (positive or negative). The readers are therefore encouraged to understand the underlying mechanism of the technique without paying much attention to its name.

Through this technique, we will try to build up the capacity to 'letting-go of thoughts' by repetitively focusing our attention back on an *anchor*. As our attention latches on the anchor, it automatically practices letting-go from distracting thoughts.

The anchor will be a word with no particular meaning, but will be capable of inducing an impactful sensation pattern in the body.

We will call this technique "Hover & Anchor." You will need to perform a quick two minutes minute prep before you perform this technique.

Preparation for "Hover & Anchor."

You should spend a couple of minutes going through this before the main session.

1. Sit in a closed room without distractions. Outdoor is not advised as part of the routine practice.

2. Be aware of your buttocks before you start. Balance your weight evenly – whether you are sitting on a mat or on a chair.

3. Try to keep your back as straight as possible.

4. Before you start, think about an image that triggers a natural outpouring of love. Image of pets or kids (when they were small) is usually very effective.

5. Think a time when you were a small kid and when you were *taken care of.* Try to experience the feeling of "I am taken care of."

6. This last prep step is a bit counter intuitive but it turbo charges the session if you can do this correctly. You need to do a self-affirmation that "I do not want anything from this session." If done with the right spirit, this helps in settling down the thoughts like "am I getting there?" or "how am I doing?" or "is this thing working after all?" These distracting thoughts can lure you in abandoning the exercise.

Mind-Gym Technique 5: Hover & Anchor

Category: Core

Sit comfortably and erect with your back straight. Close your eyes.

Now say the word "Hum" loudly. Draw this word out. Hhhaummm. The entire word should take three to five seconds. Use this drawn out version of "Hum" for this technique.

Observe the vibrations the word creates in the body. Does the "Hhha" parts cause a vibration in the abdomen – around the solar plexus area? And the 'mmm' part create vibrations in your chest, neck & head?

Now think, "Hum" without vocalizing. Observe that the vibration pattern that you observed earlier would still exist in a fainter form.

[Once you have practiced this technique a few times, you can skip the part above and directly start from this point onwards]

[Main Routine]

Set up a timer for 10 minutes.

Observe that your vocal chords are moving involuntarily - ever so lightly – even as you think about the word "Hum" – which is your anchor-thought. Get this 'thinking of Hum' to a lower volume where the involuntary movement of vocal chords is barely perceptible.

Observe the subtle sensations the anchor-thought causes in the body when you think about it. This subtle sensation combined with 'thinking of Hum' will be the anchor for your attention.

If your attention wanders into other thoughts, get it back to the anchor "Hum" *whenever you become aware of the fact that you have wandered.*

If your attention does not wander, wait for 5-6 seconds and think "Hum" again (repeat the procedure).

You may 'zone out', or move into the gap between thoughts sometime during the practice. As soon as you realize you are in the zone – bring the attention back to the anchor.

Continue this until the 10-minute timer rings. Continue sitting still with your eyes closed for one more minute before resuming other activities.

Notes:

- It may take a few days for you to settle down and feel comfortable with the exercise. Please perform this routine with as much diligence as you can because it is the main exercise of Mind-Gym.

- Breathe naturally during the exercise. Your attention will be on the anchor and not on the pattern of your breathing. The breathing may slow down and can occasionally pause.

- If your attention wanders into thoughts, bring it back to the anchor (Hum) whenever you realize it. Try not to judge or get frustrated if you wander into thoughts excessively. Even if you end up wandering into thought stories for most of the session, as long as you have the intention to come back to the anchor-thought, you will be building your mind muscles. It is very important to understand this point and therefore not *give-up.*

- Make sure that you do not think about the anchor-thought in the 'background' while the attention is still on thought stories Your attention should be sharp enough to be exclusively on the anchor in each cycle even if it wanders shortly after.

- You may feel a 'sinking' or a 'falling' feeling when you let go the thought stories and get back to the anchor. This is a common response as a result of 'letting-go' a thought stream. Gradually, you will be able to do the *letting-go* without getting this sensation.

- You may 'zone out', or move into a gap sometime during the practice. As soon as you realize you are in the zone – bring the attention back to the anchor-thought. You may feel tempted to hover around in this silent zone, but you need to come back to the anchor-thought as soon as you realize you are in the zone. This is an important instruction that needs to be closely followed for the exercise to be effective.

- Of course, you can (and will) stay in the zone as long as you *do not* realize you are there.
- It is important to note that we are *not* practicing to *stay in the zone* during the exercise. Our routine is to practice *getting back at the anchor*, as a result of which we will start experiencing the silent 'zone' naturally outside the practices.
- The anchor may become less pronounced as you gain practice. The phonetics may become altered and may just reduce to "aaaa" or '"hhhh". This stage will usually happen after the practice is a bit established.

Exercise 2: Zoning Out

You will need: A sport or exercise routine that you enjoy

You can observe this while enjoying your favorite sport or workout.

- Gently notice the absence of thoughts when you 'zone out' during the game or routine.

- Notice that this 'zone' enables you to be *one with the action* of the game. There is no *you* separate from *your game* – both become one?

Notes:

- Athletes are most productive in this zone. They also find this state the most enjoyable part of their athletic experience.

- What if this 'zone' experience could be carried on to your other daily activities at your will? Could that make these activities more enjoyable?

Assignment

Day						
1	2	3	4	5	6	7
8 ✔	9 ✔	10 ✔	11 ✔	12 ✔	13 ✔	14 ✔
15	16	17	18	19	20	21
22	23	24	25	26	27	28

1. Strengthening routines
- Belly breathing (Technique 1): As much as you can through the day.

  Mind-Gym session: This session can be done at any convenient time but at least two hours after a meal. Please perform these routines indoor in a quiet room, free from interruptions. Sit comfortably on a mat or on a chair with your back erect. Remember that regularity is key to building your mind muscles.

2. Warm-Up
*   Ten times bumblebee Humming (Technique 3)
*   20 times balanced breathing (Technique 4)

3. Core
*   Five minutes of sensation watching (Technique 2)
*   10 minutes Hover & Anchor (Technique 5)
*   One-minute rest. Close eyes, lean back or lie down.

Connecting the Dots

*   Our attention is conditioned to latch on to cue-thoughts. As our attention jumps from one cue-thought to other it *involuntarily* 'lets-go' of the last thought.
*   The Hover & Anchor technique we learned in this chapter uses a prop called anchor-thought to repeatedly move our attention from a cue-thought back to this anchor.
*   This eventually helps in recalling the moment of 'letting go' that happens in each of these cycles. This then helps our attention to *voluntarily* let-go of these (or any other) thoughts.
*   We also experienced the *zone of no thoughts* from where we can *watch* all thoughts.

THE BIG PICTURE

Some waves think they are not part of the ocean!

There is a beautiful lagoon overlooking the Blue Ocean on the western side of Oahu Island in Hawaii. Massive volcanic mountains guard a thin strip of sandy beach, their soft slopes casting an emerald shadow over the sparkling water.

In the lagoon were white corals and colorful fish. The fish were all sizes, shapes, and colors; there were purple fish, orange fish, green fish and any other color fish one could think of!

But this story is not about the green mountains, the emerald lagoon or the colorful fish. It is about

something just across the bay, deep in the Ocean –
two little waves. A small wave called Honu and his
bubbly little wave friend Meha. Honu and Meha lived
with millions of other waves in the ocean. They spent
most of their time jumping in and out of the ocean
with other small waves, making the ocean look like a
giant trampoline.

"I can't wait to become a big swell," Honu said eying
one of the big swells lazily rolling around the surface,
not too far from them.

"They say that one has to learn the language of the
winds, and follow them to faraway places before you
become big – it that true? " Meha remarked plopping
next to Honu.

"Yes that is true," Honu replied, "And don't tell anyone
... ", He added with a hushed splash," I have almost
learned the language of the winds. They say that the
seasonal winds will pass this way again very soon. I
am going to follow them!"

"I don't want you to leave me alone," Meha was almost
in tears. It was difficult to detect her anguish because
the salty tears looked pretty much like the rest of her.

"I won't. I will take you with me."

Several waves had followed the westerly winds a
short while ago. Honu had watched in admiration as

the first wave had set out on the ocean following the wind and as other waves had followed. He had been preparing for his excursion listening to the incessant splashes of the big old wise swell that ebbed around the little waves, sharing with them drops of wisdom.

"The wind takes us out on our journey – without it, we are nothing", the big old wave had said, "Never forget that." The big swell looked remarkably peaceful as it rolled around on the surface of the ocean, towering over the little waves, "Also, it gets a bit cold when the wind gets strong – put on your white caps if that happens," the old wave had said with a wink.

But the words of wisdom were forgotten as soon as the wind had picked up. The waves had scrambled out on the ocean surface with a rush of excitement. Like a giant roller coaster through the ocean – the ones on the front riding under the illusion that they were leading and the ones on the back under the illusion that they were following as the winds hauled them towards their destiny.

The westerly winds arrived shortly. It was a bright morning, and the wise old wave was telling them about stories from faraway seas when the wind had started to pick up.

"Hey! I am shining like a diamond!" a tiny ripple plopped, basking in the reflected glory of the mid-morning sun.

"Of course, you are, dear!" The wise wave did not want to dampen the enthusiasm of the small ripple, "You must see the waves near the emerald lagoon which is just down the horizon, though," he continued as he patiently rolled around the restless ripples. " I have heard that the waves there look like red rubies!"

"How can a wave look red?" Meha had wondered, but she was too shy to ask. Both Meha and Honu were less than a day old – very young in wave years. They had not yet seen a sunset. Just then the winds picked up again. "Follow me, "Honu shouted at Meha as they set out to the open sea. Meha followed Honu and along with many other ripples, started speeding up towards the horizon.

———— ❧ ————

"Do red waves really exist?" Meha asked Honu as they glided through the ocean surface. She had been wondering about what the old wave had said just before they set out.

"You don't believe in the old wave's stories, do you," Honu laughed, "He is mad. Blue waves, yellow waves, even green waves I can imagine. But how in the name of floating kelp can a wave be red?"

Honu laughed as he swelled with the wind – he was getting bigger. They cruised along for a few more hours. The winds were picking up. "The old wave did talk sense sometimes - like putting up the white caps "Meha mumbled, putting up hers. She liked the old wise wave - his quiet roll was different from the restless ripples surrounding her.

"Ha! Everyone knows about white caps," Honu shouted above the wind "How about other rubbish he talks about - like all of us being connected? You, me and every other wave being just a small part of the ocean ... do you remember that? That old wave – I tell you - it's time for him to evaporate."

"How do you know he is wrong?" Meha protested.

"Everyone knows that he is wrong," Honu looked offended "We are all waves ... supported by this ocean ... which in turn is supported by the huge Turtle" Honu smirked, "And that Turtle is supported by another ... and it goes on ... it is as simple as that"

A faint outline of a shore appeared far away near the horizon, and with it a swarm of pelicans that glided noisily past them.

"Watch out," Meha shouted as a pelican dived towards Honu. Before Honu could realize, the bird crashed through his ebbing form as he watched them in disbelief. His quiet disbelief turned into horror as the pelican reappeared with a squirming anchovy in its beak.

"The old wave did say that there are treasures hidden in the ocean- just beneath the waves," Meha said excitedly.

———⟨❦⟩———

It was getting dark, and the familiar blue sky had started to turn orange. The distant shore was getting closer and closer as mossy green mountains loomed above them. They could see the waves ahead of them crashing into a big reef that guarded an emerald lagoon.

"That old wave...", Honu's voice was laced with apprehension as he saw the fate of the waves crashing ahead " Do you think he was right?", he looked back at Meha who was following him, "that there are treasures hidden in the ocean- just beneath us."

Meha gave a sparkling smile, "Let's find out!" She embraced Honu in an affectionate hug and together, they dipped their heads under the surface.

MIND-GYM SESSION FIVE

How about we do a quick recap of what unboxing is really about? Simply put, it is all about seeing things with minimal influence of our stored cue-thoughts. This new type of seeing enables us to engage with action-thoughts more effectively. It enables us to think only when we want to.

In this session we will perform exercises to explore how much of the overall picture do we miss because of the pattern of our thoughts?

Exercise 1: Seeing through the Box

Read the poem THE BOXED MEN AND THE OX from Chapter 3 "The Box"

Reflect on why the Boxed could not see the Ox.

- Can you recall specific instances where you made incorrect inferences when initially you were absolutely certain that these inferences were correct?

Exercise 2: Seeing through the Box
You will need: A smartphone or laptop with Internet.

YouTube search keywords: 'Selective Attention test'

There should be many videos that come up. Select one that has most views. The video will be of a basketball game where you will be asked to track a specific object as players play the game.

Notes:

- Did you get the right count?
- Did you notice the "surprise"?
- What do feel about the kind of attention that can count the number of passes accurately and also notices the "surprise"?

- Can you relate this attention to the one you experienced in Exercise 1 of Mind-Gym Session1?
- How do you think our attention is naturally wired for survival? How often do you feel a chill shoot up your spine based on "false triggers"?

The box that hinders our ability to see the big picture is itself imperceptible. Regular practice of *Hover & Anchor*, will gradually make this Box perceptible. As we have more and more awareness of the zone of no thoughts, or the gap between the thoughts, we will be on our way to cutting eyeholes in the Box.

But there is one more thing that we can do right now to *feel* the box.

Mind-Gym Technique 6: Feel the Box.
Category: Strengthening routine

This technique needs just a two minutes. You can perform this as often as you wish to, several times in a day. This technique is helpful in temporarily reducing the *'heaviness'* of the box.

If you can sit down, please do so. You do not need to close your eyes. Scan your body for any sensation of discomfort.

These sensations will be spread across the body - mainly across head, face, upper and lower back, chest, and abdomen. If you feel pains due to any chronic or temporary medical condition, please include that too in your attention.

Pay more attention to any contraction, pricking, throbbing, tingling, heaviness, churning, or similar sensations in the head, chest or abdomen. Use the skill that you have developed via Mind-Gym Technique 2: Watching Sensations to do this.

By paying attention to these sensations, you are *feeling* the box. Most of the unpleasant sensations in the body rise *because* of the Box. These are our cue-thoughts way of trying to communicate with our attention.

Remain attentive about these sensations for two minutes *without judging them*. Try not to judge the sensations as good or bad. Bring your attention back to the sensations if you drift into thought stories.

At the end of two minutes, take three belly breaths and carry on with your regular work.

Assignment

Day						
1	2	3	4	5	6	7
8	9	10	11	12	13	14
15 ✓	16 ✓	17 ✓	18 ✓	19 ✓	20 ✓	21 ✓
22	23	24	25	26	27	28

1. Strengthening routines
- Belly breathing (Technique 1):As much as you can.
- Feel the box (Technique 6) at the end of your lunch or coffee/tea breaks.

2. Keep a watch on at least one strong emotion that gets triggered during the day. Welcome this opportunity (even if the emotion is not pleasant) to watch the sensations this emotion caused.

Mind-Gym session:

3. Warm-Up
- 10 times bumblebee humming (Technique 3)
- 20 times balanced breathing (Technique 4)

4. Core
- Five minutes of sensation watching (Technique 2)
- 10 minutes Hover & Anchor (Technique 5)
- One-minute rest. Close eyes, lean back or lie down.

Connecting the Dots

- We explored how the Box limits our ability to perceive reality by influencing our attention.
- We learned how to 'Feel the Box' by paying attention to the sensations in our body.
- These sensations are the hidden doorway through which we can *see* and eventually diffuse the cue-thoughts that form the Box.

> - Using a combination of 'letting-go' of image part of the cue-thought and the 'watching' the sensations part of them gives us two alternatives to limit its power to influence our attention.

STORY OF AN ELEPHANT

Some elephants in this world were unhappy because they were trying to act like Giraffes!

The little princess was wandering through the enchanted woods when she heard a strange voice. The princess always loved the wonderful surprises that the forest had in store and smiled in anticipation.

"Hello, there!" came a disembodied voice, like a sound squeezed through a thin pipe. "Hello there!" came the voice again.

The princess traced her gaze to the source of the voice and saw a ferret standing on a branch of tree– just at her eye level.

"Hey it's me here!" the ferret said, waving its arms, "You can call me Aunt ferret if you want to – I should be the age of your Aunt in ferret years, " she said smiling, "I haven't seen you in this part of the woods", the ferret looked at the princess who had an amazed expression on her face.

"You know, I am new to this place as well", the ferret continued before the princess could respond," I used to live in a house. In a big wooden box with a big ferret wheel. Then one day I realized that I was not happy."

"There was another ferret on that wheel", she squeaked, "and we used to chase each other", the ferret winked.

"We used to run because we loved running. Oh the arch of the feet! The graceful swish of the tail! A perfect stride! "the ferret sighed rolling her eyes.

"And then one day both of us realized that we were no longer running because we loved to run. We were now running just to stay ahead of each other. That was the day we stepped out of the wheel", the ferret paused.

"Sorry ... I am doing all the talking! " Aunt ferret looked at the princess. The brief pause amplified the silence of the woods.

"I love to listen", the princess smiled.

"Let me tell you a funny thing, "the ferret continued, holding a giggle and twitching her pink nose "We had been so busy running on the wheel that we did not notice that the box was not locked!" the ferret chuckled.

"Did you see anything interesting? After you had got out of the box?" the little princess asked.

"You bet. There are more wonders in this world than one can expect! Come, let me show you some of them. Just follow me."

<hr>

They walked leisurely through a winding trail. Just after a thick grove of bamboo, the trail went through a clearing. An elephant was dozing at the center of the clearing, lying on his belly with his arms and legs outstretched. His face was towards the trail, the trunk vibrating with his loud snores.

A little Bee was perched proudly on the Elephant's right ear, with a tiny black object in her right hand. The object looked like a miniature microphone. She held a piece of paper in her left hand, sporting a long white judges wig, as she stood supported by her four legs, with a smug expression on her face.

"Here starts our adventure. Meet the sad Elephant and the judge Bee. She is always judging you see – it is a Bee that would not let anything to just – BE", Aunt Ferret whispered under her breath. "Whatever you do not engage her in a conversation. Because once she gets started, it is tough to stop her..."

But Aunt Ferret's warning came a fraction of a second too late, "Hey what is that in your hand?" the little Princess had already asked the bee.

"It is a micro-microphone," a strange squeaky but excited voice boomed in the clearing, " A *picophone*," the Bee smiled, smugly pleased with the pun.

"Do you know that I am not just any other judge? I am a *magnificent* judge! Thought. J. Bee. That is my name. And you know, I am very close to winning an Oscar..."

Before the Little Princess could reply, the bee had opened up the piece of paper in her hand. "Here, listen to my Oscar acceptance speech," she said excitedly. Then she started narrating a poem in an animated singsong voice:

"My life is Hollywood blockbuster, ye fellas'
Better than your life, just watch it and get jealous!

A camera hides somewhere outside of me,

As I live my life through what the camera can see.

This camera changes hands without making me wary,
From my family to my friends, colleagues and often an
adversary!

Fantastic performance, superb acting, my friends say,
and I concur,
And one day I will surely win that coveted Oscar!!"

The bee clapped her hands excitedly and then took a
bow. Her clapping, amplified by the Pico phone,
echoed across the clearing.

"I did not imagine a small little bee could create such a
noise," the little princess mumbled, when suddenly
she noticed that the dozing elephant stirred slightly
and opened one of his eyes. Then raising himself
groggily he sat on its hind legs with the front legs
stretched ahead at an awkward angle. The elephant's
eyes gradually focused as he sat on the ground staring
at Aunt ferret and the little princess.

"What is your name?" the little princess asked the
elephant politely.

"*A human no different from more or less the entire*
humanity," he mumbled, " That is my name. I know it
sounds funny, almost unbelievable but it is true. We
elephants like to keep crazy and long names. What is
your name?'

"I don't have a name – I am called *Little Princess* by my friends," the princess replied back smiling.

———◦◦◦———

The elephant then narrated his story to the little princess and Aunt ferret as the bee stood on his right ear with the usual smug expression on her face.

"I used to be a happy Elephant - roaming around freely in the forest, then one day this bee landed on my ear," the elephant said pointing at the bee with his trunk.

"She promised me that she would make my life better if I started believing in her judgments. She will keep me away from harm's way, but she lied to me.

The Bee no longer lets me *be*. Thought J Bee. I later found out that her middle initial stood for Judge. She is an *always-judging* bee.

It started out with harmless judgments. I like this, and I don't like this. Then the drama became more and more complicated. Including craving, aversion, and jealousy. Once the Bee gets going, she sucks me into the drama. And before I realize, I am in her story matching her narrative with my feelings. Which for me always ends in suffering.

Judging things – Judging others – Judging myself. The Bee tells me stories about an imaginary camera that I need to *act out to*", the elephant had a somber expression.

"Act out what?" Little Princess asked.

"She wants me to act like a Giraffe!" the elephant said as tears welled up in his eyes.

"You fool, do you even know why I want you to act like a Giraffe? Giraffe is the tallest animal on the planet. So Giraffe is better than Elephant," Judge Bee's melodramatic rant boomed through the clearing.

"I beg your pardon - but elephant is the largest land animal on the planet," little princess interrupted the bee, "and the strongest," she continued, " Why would an elephant ever want to be a giraffe?"

The bee's face turned red, and she started reading another poem in the picophone.

"One beautiful day it dawned on me
Life at this moment as I experience, hear and see,
Is perhaps not what it used to be?

But this moment doesn't really matter, I must say,

As I fully utilize my present in two ways,
To plan for tomorrow as I mull over yesterday.

"Now *you* sing this," she instructed the elephant through the picophone, "otherwise bad things will happen to you - dreadful things," her voice had a threatening tone.

The elephant brought his trunk near little princess' ears and whispered, "She tells me things like this throughout the day - that is the reason I am so sad," tears were again rolling down his cheek.

"Why don't you tell her that what she is saying is not right? ", the little princess asked the elephant

"I tried – but she gets red-faced and angry and shouts more loudly."

"Why don't you just flap your ears and squish her?" little princess asked.

"Do you think I did not try? She is very fast and just flies away!" the elephant started wailing again, "Thought J Bee has hijacked my life! How do I stop the noise of this pest perched on my head?"

By this time, Judge Bee was already reciting her tenth poem on the picophone.

Aunt ferret, who had been quiet for all this time whispered to the little princess "We need to do something about this elephant – what was his name – *A Human no different from more or less the entire Humanity* ... and I think I have a plan!"

Aunt ferret had then hopped up to a branch close to the elephant's left ear and whispered something into it. A spark of excitement flashed across the elephant's eyes.

———— ❧ ————

"What did you whisper in the elephant's ear?" the little princess asked Aunt Ferret as they made their way through the lush green canopy.

"A small trick," Aunt Ferret replied. "The trick is very useful in getting rid of annoying bees like the one we just met," she said with a twinkle in her eyes.

"The trick is very simple - look at the Thought bee every time it speaks.", she said with a giggle.

"It seems very simple ... are you sure it works?" little princess asked. Aunt ferret nodded.

"It is indeed simple, but here is the tricky part," she paused looking at the beautiful eyes of the little princess, "One should say nothing to the Bee - not a word - just look at the bee without judging the judge. This *not judging the judge* part may take some practice."

"What practice?"

"Sit quietly and let go of the impressions created by the Bee. The images it conjures, the sensations it creates. Do this every day. And one day you will find that you are free from it's trap. Trust me – it works."

———— ✦ ————

Suddenly the trails gave way to lush opening with light green grass swaying gently in the wind. Beyond the dancing meadow were huge mountains overlooking the forest.

The sun shone through the clouds illuminating the outline of mossy green mountains that curved around them in a near perfect arch. The arch of mountains overlooked an azure blue ocean. Two waterfalls cascaded from cliffs around them. One from their left and other from their right. These waterfalls tumbled down into a meandering stream that merged into the ocean in the horizon. They settled down on a patch of grass overlooking the beautiful sight.

Their conversation was interrupted by a loud crash. The noise came from the dense forest across the meadows. One of the trees that stood guarding the edge of the forest shook violently, and we saw our elephant emerge from under it, making his way towards them.

"I followed your tracks, " he said panting. His eyes had a strange twinkle that I had not noticed before.

The sad elephant was happy!

The bee was still sitting on his right ear with her usual smug expression. Her lips were moving animatedly, but they could not hear what she was saying. Then the little princess realized that her picophone was missing.

'Thank you!" the elephant said sheepishly to Aunt ferret. "I looked at the bee every time she spoke," he giggled, "She challenged me to say something when I looked at her - but I did not - and to my surprise she threw the picophone away!" The elephant said excitedly, "I can finally do what I want to do!"

"Now that the thought bee no longer controls your life - you can put her to perform some real work. I have heard that they are the best in making honey," Aunt ferret winked.

And at that moment, when the bee had no longer hijacked the elephant's attention, he noticed a magnificent valley right in front of him as a smile spread across his face.

MIND-GYM SESSION SIX

We have explored how cue-thoughts lure our attention and prevent us from working efficiently. These thoughts also impact our capacity to relax by luring us into doing unnecessary actions.

We have also seen how watching the thoughts and feelings (expressed as sensations in our body) helps us in not getting pulled into the thought stories and therefore remaining in the 'zone' of expanded attention.

Let's now explore this zone a bit more. This zone is the gateway to true creativity, intelligence and compassion. This zone is known by many names: presence, mindfulness and such. What it is called by is not important. What is important is that we are able to feel it naturally.

Exercise 1: Exploring the Zone
You will need: A timer with alarm.

Three minutes of sensation watching

Five times Bumblebee Humming

Ten times balanced breathing

[Prepare for first round of *Hover & Anchor*]

In the session, try to notice the space *just after* you become aware that you have drifted in a thought stream and have started to get back to the anchor-thought 'Hum.'

This space happens *between* the cue-thought and the "Hum" thought. It will be a fleeting moment, and it is OK if you are not able to observe this initially. Just have an intention for your attention to *see* this space eventually.

[Prepare for a second round of *Hover & Anchor*]

Try to be aware of the space between *two consecutive* anchor-thoughts. This is the 'pause' before you pick up the next repetition of the anchor-thought. This is the gap between the thoughts. This is a zone where there are no thoughts.

What does this zone feel like?

Notes:

- What happens when you try to observe the zone? Does it go away?
- This zone of *no thoughts* is similar to the zone experience during sports. Imagine how it would be to be in this zone, at will, with your eyes open, during routine daily activities.

With practice, this zone will gradually become more pervasive, spilling into your daily activities.

Mind-Gym Technique7: Mindful Eating

Sit in a quiet place during your next meal. Chew the first five bites 32 times.

Use the taste and the sensations in your mouth as the anchor if you drift away into thoughts. Come back to these sensations whenever you become aware you have drifted into thoughts.

Mind-Gym Technique 8: Mindful Walking

Sit comfortably on a chair.

Watch the sensations in your arms and legs. Start with right leg, then right arm, left arm and then left leg. Spend about one minute in each section.

Now spend a minute trying to be aware of *all* the sensations of your body at the same time. End the session with five belly breaths.

Now walk in a quiet place. You can start by walking around inside your house and then (weather permitting) move outdoors around your backyard or lawn.

While walking, try to be aware of the sensations of your whole body. Initially, you may need to restrict your attention to a part of your body sensations, but with practice you will be able to be aware of *all* the body sensations at the same time. To start with, you can use sensations of any particular part of your body – your face, tip of your nose, your chest, etc.

Use your body sensation as an anchor when you realize that your attention had drifted away into thoughts.

Be aware of the thoughts you may find yourself engaged during the walk. Be aware of thoughts like "this looks so good/bad" or "this is so lovely/awful." Be aware when you compare the surrounding with another experience - from another time or another place. Bring your attention back to the sensations and enjoy the walk.

Once you are comfortable with the technique, try to walk mindfully all the time especially when you are close to the nature.

Notes:

- Did you feel you were in the 'zone' during your walk?
- Did you have difficulty in walking when you were in this zone?
- Were you absent-minded in this zone? Or more Alert? Check this out during your next mindful walking session.

Assignment

Day						
1	2	3	4	5	6	7
8	9	10	11	12	13	14
15	16	17	18	19	20	21
✔22	✔23	✔24	✔25	✔26	✔27	✔28

1. Strengthening routines
- Belly breathing (Technique 1): As much as you can.
- Feel the box (Technique 6) before every important meeting and after every work break.
- Mindfully eat (Technique 7), at least four bites in each meal.
- Mindfully walk (Technique 8), for at least ten minutes every day.

Mind-Gym session:

2. Warm-Up
  - 10 times bumblebee Humming (Technique 3)
  - 20 times balanced breathing (Technique 4)

3. Core
- Five minutes of sensation watching (Technique 2)
- 10 minutes Hover & Anchor (Technique 5)
- One-minute rest. Close eyes, lean back or lie down.

Connecting the Dots

- Our introduction to *zone of no thoughts* happens through the gap between the thoughts. This gap is the metaphorical hole in the box of thoughts.
- We first explored this gap experientially through the *Exploring Attention* exercise of Mind-Gym Session One. We later got a deeper glimpse of it through the anchor techniques.

- When this gap becomes bigger and pervasive we have our eyeholes through which we can see beyond the box.
- Our attention has a different quality in the zone. It is an expansive place from where we can watch the thoughts without engaging with them.
- We can be fully functional and much more effective from this zone.
- We also noted that this zone could be extended to our daily activities like walking, eating, and sports.
- This zone of silence eventually enables us to *see* the trick to evolve the *way we think*.

This zone also gives us the ability to connect the dots of this fascinating journey on our own.

THE THOUGHT-FACTORY

It's time to take a look inside the factory where our attention and our thoughts interact!

A s we continue our journey, exploring the realm of thoughts and attention, the cue-thoughts gradually become less effective in luring our attention. Our attention which used be overwhelmed by these cues, now frees up to observe the movement of these thoughts. When this happens, we will be able to dive deeper into the metaphorical thought-factory where all this action is taking place.

This factory is where the play between our attention and thoughts takes place. This is where thoughts are created. So what is happening in this factory?

A stream of cue-thoughts designated to distract our attention line up outside a mysterious gate in the thought-factory.

Our attention stands on the other side of the door.

The Thought Weaver

If we could peep inside that door, we would find a huge room filled up with machines. These machines would come in different shapes and sizes - some small some big, some new some old. In this metaphorical world, we would also see our *attention* as a cartoon character, representing the invisible center of all my experiences.

We would find that these machines started working as soon as attention touched them. They then spun out a stream of action-thoughts, which were then used by us to perform actions.

Let's call these 'action-thought spinning machines,' *thought weavers*. Every thought weaver in the factory would spin out action-thoughts after *attention* pushes its start button.

But how does our attention choose a particular thought weaver? Here lies the key point that we have identified as the source of 'bad thinking.'

The cue-thoughts influence the choice of thought weaver. They point our attention towards a thought weaver that is wired to handle a particular cue-thought.

The Pattern Matcher

Even when all this action is taking place, another part of the thought-factory is furiously busy, continuously processing inputs from our senses.

As soon as this part of the factory, lets call it the *pattern matcher*, 'gathers' information from our senses, unknown to our attention, it sends a train of cue-thoughts towards the gate we saw earlier.

These cue-thoughts are served based on match of the 'present' with any of the *similar past situations* in the cue-thought archives. Cue-thoughts then arrive one by one through the gate and point to a thought weaver associated with the cue.

This mechanism works irrespective of the fact whether I am doing any focused work or just idling or resting. The cue-thought pattern matching happens automatically and continuously. This matching does not care whether I am trying to work or trying to take a break from it. Let's explore this with an example.

Curious case of a pet hunt

I am working from my home office, comfortably perched on a leather chair, peering into a MacBook. I have just finished preparing for an important office event scheduled tomorrow.

I am very close to wrapping up my work, and then suddenly something strange happens. I get a surge of apprehension and instead of finishing off the work, I start checking and re-checking what I had completed so far. Then out of the blue I see a flash of an accident that happened sixteen years ago. Slightly distracted, I take a deep breath and focus back. Then I feel a feeling of fear rising within me.

"Did I lock the backyard door?" a thought flashes in my mind, "I hope Kitty did not get out of the house, "I intone these words. Then dropping what I was doing, I rush out of the study looking for my pet cat.

You raise your eyebrows questioningly, wondering about this seemingly irrational behavior.

This apparently inconsistent behavior was because of the activities that happened in my thought-factory. Let's now pick up a magnifying glass and dive into the factory to examine what prompted this sequence of actions.

My attention had been busy formulating action-thoughts preparing for tomorrow's important event. My senses were fully active as my attention was entirely focused.

In a small little gap during my sensing, much subtle than I could perceive, as I checked through the list of activities that I had already reviewed with my boss earlier today, my attention moved from the activities to the image of my boss.

At this moment, unknown to me, there was an automatic pattern matching with all my past experiences with the boss. And then the results came in from the depths of my mind-body with all past events where I had fallen short of his expectations. A cue-thought knocked on my attention. This one had a faint apprehension as it's feeling component. The image was from a past occurrence where I had my knuckles tapped for making a mistake.

I abandoned the thread of my original focused good thinking and had looped into checking and re-checking my already complete work. My focus now shifted from completing the work to making sure that I am eventually appreciated by my boss for all the hard work I had done.

It is a totally new event that is scheduled tomorrow where a lot unknown things could happen despite best preparations. What if I was unable to handle these unknown things? Unknown to me, my attention had now moved from finishing what *I could actually do* to worrying about things that were beyond my control.

The wired response for unknown situations like this is a feeling of fear and there is a unique cue-thought: "Cue ID#1: Fear of Unknown". This was one of the oldest cue-thoughts in our thought-factory.

So even as I was right on the threshold of completing my work, CUE ID#1 walks into the door of the factory and points towards an ancient thought weaver.

The cue is wearing a label of fear due to which, a feeling of fear appears through its unique pattern of sensations in my body. The much familiar sensation of fear gets my attention to acknowledge this uninvited cue-thought. My attention then notices that the cue-thought is pointing towards an ancient thought weaver.

That one ?
OK ! I will be right there !!

My attention then moves towards this ancient but frequently used thought weaver that was made tens of millenniums ago. Attention then activates the start button of this weaver.

Before we go further, let's pause for a moment and cast our much familiar *good thinking* and *bad thinking* from the context of this thought-factory.

Good Thinking vs. Bad Thinking

The ability of my attention to operate a thought weaver, spinning out effective action-thoughts followed by effective action is 'good thinking.'

Getting lured by cue-thoughts and unknowingly switching over to a different thought weaver, resulting in action-thoughts followed by actions that are not optimal is 'bad thinking.'

Continuing our exploration, I observe that there are thousands of thought weavers in the factory. I notice that a lot of these machines had been installed during my school education. Then there were many that had come bundled with my college degrees.

Just like we install or update applications on our smartphones, every time I learned or upgraded a skill, a new thought weaver was installed or an older version was updated.

But then there were many thought weavers that I could not recognize. They came from sources I was unaware of. These looked old and primitive like the one CUE#1 was pointing to.

My attention, surprisingly, never questioned these mysterious thought weavers despite the fact that many of them produced illogical, irrelevant, and sometimes dangerous set of action-thoughts.

Workings of a strange factory

Let's now have a closer look at the ancient thought weaver that CUE#1 had pointed to. The cue-thought has already activated "fear" related sensations in my body (because 'fear' was included under the 'feeling' part of the cue). These sensations had in turn drawn my attention to the cue. A sequence of activities happens now.

The feeling of fear expressed in my body, draws a bunch of other cue-thoughts that also have "fear" encoded as their sensation. This is enabled by another hidden mechanism embedded in our mind-body fabric.

Though the first cue was *somewhat* related to the current situation, all these secondary cues have *little or no correlation* to what is happening right now. All they have in common is the emotion of 'fear'. All these cue thoughts that share this common element of 'fear' then line up outside the gate to attract my attention to hear out their stories.

This is the main reason why the messages these cue-thoughts convey appear to be random and mostly unrelated to the current situation.

All 'Fear' related seed thoughts please proceed to thought interruption Gate #1 !

So what can we do about this? The practice of watching our sensations gives us the ability to render a cue-thought trigger ineffective. *If we can watch the sensation that a cue-thought created without getting entangled with it, we stop the flow of all the subsequent ones who stand queued up waiting for their turn.*

So if we 'watch' the emotion of fear as it expresses itself through sensations in the body, the sensations will eventually recede, and the assembled cue-thoughts would be dismissed.

Sent back this way, these cue-thoughts loose a part of their power. Next time they appear, the emotion they serve will be fainter - giving our attention a better chance to be able to let-go of this weaker cue.

Story of a thought weaver

In our example, a group of 'Fear' related cue-thoughts assemble and express themselves one at a time. One of these fear cues is from a car accident that happened sixteen years ago. This cue-thought's fear inducing capacity has diminished over time but is still strong enough to flash in my mind. But the cue is not strong enough to alter my intention. Then another cue with a much more powerful impression comes along.

All these 'Fear' cues are programmed to point to an ancient thought weaver that specializes in *handling fear*. So what does it do?

This weaver runs on a seemingly simple logic that is based on the *image or visual* provided to it by the cue-thought. We have explored this visual in sufficient depth and therefore will be quite familiar with it.

This visual is a summary of my experience when the cue thought had been created and at its basic level includes either something that I crave for (or like), or I have an aversion to (or dislike).

The logic followed by thought weaver once it captures this visual is roughly as such:

1. If the visual is of something that I like, check if I own it. If I do, then make sure that I do not lose it.
2. If the visual is of something that I do not like, make sure I do not end up owning it.

You may find it fascinating that this simple logic is generally applicable to all situations of fear. You can check it out with some examples from your own life and verify this.

The various cue-thoughts that have now lined up to attract my attention are all from a past experience of fear, and each has its own visual or image related to the fear sensation. One of them was created when I was a boy, and had lost my pet cat.

A cue-thought's power lies in its ability to induce the feeling that is coded within it - this feeling is what catches our attention. Also, the capability of producing the emotion (and hence grabbing our attention) grows as a particular cue is used more often.

This can be felt experientially with respect to cue-thought triggers that correspond to addictive behaviors. Once our attention starts 'servicing' these thoughts, the action thoughts (and therefore action) become increasingly wired and predictable.

So as we can see now, the set of actions that are now getting triggered in my mind have nothing to do with the work that I was originally performing. These actions were now about *handling a feeling* – feeling of fear in this case, using a cue from a past experience.

Let's now observe the sequence of events that happen next.

1. The cues start coming through the door, one at a time, luring my attention from my work related thought weaver, towards the ancient 'Handle fear' thought weaver. My attention checks these cues out. It ignores the ones that induce a weak sensation of fear – like the one from my car accident. However the image contained in the cue still flashes in my mind, momentarily disturbing what I was doing. So I 'see' these cues but manage not *do* what they are asking my attention to.

2. Then a cue with a particularly 'powerful' energy arrives. This was created when I had lost my cat and had spent half a day in panic searching for her. This is also something that is currently relevant in my life because I own a cat. The visual had something I recognize – a lost cat. My attention moves to 'Handle fear' thought weaver and pushes its button.

3. "Make sure you do not lose it " the action-thought is triggered by the cue that has an image of Kitty and feeling of fear.

4. I drop everything and start acting on this new set of action-thoughts. I had to make sure that I did not lose something that I loved.

This how my thought-factory that was working on finishing up a focused activity, made me drop everything and start looking for my cat around the house. This of course is just an example, but most of our thought related *interruptions* would follow a similar pattern.

So to summarize, the cue-thoughts interrupt our actions and divert our focus to *'handle a feeling'* class of primitive thought weaver using an incident from the past as bait.

Feelings related of *fear* and *greed* are typically most potent in capturing our attention and setting it to a new course. The fear and greed related thought weavers have (roughly) the following logic:

Actions triggered by 'Fear' related cue-thoughts: Make sure that I don't lose things that I like. Make sure that I don't get things that I don't like.

Actions triggered by 'Greed' related cue-thoughts: Make sure that I get more of things I like. Make sure I have less of thing I don't like.

These *new* action thoughts are the starting point of bad thinking.

About Judgments

We carry cue-thoughts somewhere in our mind-body. These cues are the root of all our habitual pattern based behaviors, including our addictions.

These 'distractions' would not occur if my attention had the ability not to get engaged by cue-thoughts.

This is why we continue to focus on how to *handle these cue-thoughts* – rather than trying to establish the exact mechanism of how they are stored or retrieved. *Therefore the examples used in this chapter need to considered as metaphorical models and not as empirical maps.*

So how do we handle these distracting cue-thoughts? I am pretty sure that you now know the answer. In the ideal case, my attention would just look at this arriving stream of visitors, give each a polite acknowledgment and continue whatever it doing earlier. It would *not judge* these cue-thoughts even as it acknowledges them.

If I do this correctly, the sensation expressed by the cue-thought would linger around for some time and then the entire thought with its shadow of sensation would dissolve!

The *lingering time* can vary based on the intensity of the sensation and the purity of *non-judgment* during our watching of the sensation. So a Mind-Gym beginner may take several minutes to dissolve an average intensity sensation, where as a seasoned unboxed mindGymmer may be able to dissolve these sensations in a few seconds.

Not judging the arriving cue-thoughts, especially the emotion heavy ones, takes practice. This is the part that often frustrates the Mind-Gym beginners who are training to become masters of this art. But with practice our attention will be able to watch the cues without labeling them as good or bad.

Can you *see* that these cue-thoughts, in a way, are all little 'Judgments' that are cleverly summarized for future use?

Cue-thoughts are created from our past experiences. Every time we have judged something or someone knowingly or unknowingly, we have created a brief summary of our judgment in the form of these cues.

Unknown to us, these judgments remain in the mysterious realms of our mind-body, revealed only when they interrupt our thought-factory at an appropriate time.

All judgments from the past stem from two very basic judgments:

1. I *like* this thing, this person or this stuff about myself
2. I *do not like* this thing, this person or this stuff about myself.

These judgments then consolidate over time taking on different flavors. Beginning with craving and aversion (which are directly correlated to basic judgment of liking and disliking) they gradually acquire more complex shades. Almost all our emotions and feelings stem out of an initial judgment of liking or disliking.

For example, I hated someone in the past, the judgment of 'hate' stays encoded as a cue with the image of the person and a feeling of hate waiting to spring up at a later time when I see that (or similar looking) person again.

Our practice with the anchor-thought 'Hum,' develops the ability for our attention to 'let go' the cue-thoughts without judging them. This technique develops our ability to let-go the image (or mental talk) heavy thoughts with ease.

If we can watch the sensation that a cue-thought creates without getting entangled, it counts as non-judging. Thus the practice of watching the sensations gives us an additional level of skill to let-go the sensation heavy cue thoughts.

Please note that judging these cues (each of which is a summary of a judgment made in the past) – by either defending, negating or even trying to assess their logic is a sure-shot way to engage with them. You may recall this from the advice Aunt ferret gave to the Little Princess:

"A small trick," Aunt Ferret replied. "The trick is very useful in getting rid of annoying bees like the one we just met," she said with a twinkle in her eyes.

"The trick is very simple - look at the Thought bee every time it speaks", she said with a giggle.

"It seems very simple ... are you sure it works?" little princess asked. Aunt ferret nodded.

"It is indeed simple, but here is the tricky part," she paused looking at the beautiful eyes of the little princess, "One should say nothing to the Bee - not a word - just look at the bee without judging the judge. This *not judging the judge* part may take some practice."

MIND-GYM SESSION SEVEN

I In this session, we are going to learn techniques that explore Judgments.

Exercise 1: Pattern of Judgments
You will need: A timer with alarm.

Make a quiet resolve that you will *not* suppress any spontaneous judgment that arises within you. You will *judge without any guilt.* Put labels and tags to anything that you feel like. Now perform this *guilt free judging* during a five to ten-minute activity of your choice. Please make sure you do minimal talking during this activity.

> After you have done this, sit quietly for two minutes, suspend your judgments and watch the sensations in your body.

Notes:

• Were you able to identify a pattern in your judgment? What were they more about - persons, things or yourself?
• Did you feel 'good' when you were judging in wild abandon? Or were you exhausted and drained?
• Judging initially seems exciting with can be perceived as a good feeling but eventually leaves you feeling drained because it consumes a lot of your energy.

> Exercise 2: An experience without Judgments
>
> This is a thought exercise:
>
> Will you be able to enjoy something (or some activity) you like if you had not made a judgment that you *like* it? How would the experience feel like?

Notes:

• If you live through an experience that you like without judging it, the experience will always remain fresh - as if you were enjoying it for the first time. This makes the experience far more enjoyable!

- This logic applies to unpleasant experiences as well. You will be able to face them without generating unnecessary anxiety.

If you can follow these two tips, you will create fewer *new* cue-thoughts as you live through pleasant and unpleasant experiences of your life.

Mind-Gym Technique 9: Watching the Judgments
Category: Strengthening Routine

This technique helps to reduce the impact of an already created cue-thought. The basic method is to *revisit* the moments when a cue was created and then "re-live" the experience. This time we "re-live" the experience without judging.

Sit comfortably with your eyes closed.

Think about the activities of today starting from now. You will most likely recall the parts that made an impact in your mind, just move backward from now rewinding to the time you got up from the bed.

For each of the parts that you "re-live," watch them passively in you mind almost as if it was happening to somebody else. This part is critical for untangling or "diffusing" the action-thought.

You may feel the emotions that you experienced in these past events – positive or negative – but you will not judge these feelings.

Just watch the sensations and look at the images to the best of your ability. If the emotions and sensations overwhelm you, take a pause; let the emotions to naturally subside before resuming again.

If you do this well – you would have *diffused* the cue-thoughts that you created during the time you revisited in the exercise.

These cues will now be far less powerful and in some cases may even lose their hold completely.

Notes:

- How are you feeling after the re-wind? If you have done this technique properly, you should feel very close to the way you did when you got up from the bed today morning.
- This is a very useful Mind-Gym technique and can be used to reduce the impact of specific stressful events that color your routine thinking. This technique should be practiced only after you have sufficient experience of the 'gap' between thoughts. Staying in touch with that gap while re-living the experience is the most efficient way to diffuse these powerful cue-thoughts.

Letting go in silence

Now we will introduce a major core technique that extends the skill of anchoring into our day-to-day life.

Remember the quirky play that introduced the concept of anchor thoughts? And the part where Ms. Attention finally sees the fact that *she* was holding on to the thoughts and it was not the other way around. There is part of the skit, which I quote again:

> *Ms. Attention: I see it now! That cue-thought was not catching me. I was clinging on to it. And I can leave it whenever I want to!*
>
> *[The angry cue-thought extends its arms towards Ms. Attention. Ms. Attention runs close to it, barely touching its extended arms and then run back to the center of the stage with a smile on your face]*

We now know that the center of the stage is the zone of expanded awareness. It is the zone that we should have already *seen* by now in the course of our journey so far.

This space is revealed by the gap between the thoughts and is the space from where our attention can be aware of thoughts without entangling with them.

"OK, fine", you respond, "I have seen how this zone feels like during the exercises – but how do I stay in touch with this zone in my day-to-day life?"

For that, you will need to practice to *barely touch the distracting cue-thoughts and settle back into the zone.* Once you have mastered this skill you can move from any thought to this zone with ease.

We are now going to build the ability to let go thoughts further using a technique where we will *generate* a faint thought and then practice letting go of it.

This technique needs to be practiced only after there is some amount of stability and comfort with the Hover & Anchor technique.

Here we practice with a small set of self generated positive thoughts to develop the skill to let go of any cue-thought that we may sense during our daily activities.

Mind-Gym Technique 10: Thought to Zone

Category: Core

Sit comfortably with your eyes closed.

Pick one of the following as your thought. You can 'imagine' these in the form of words, image or feeling.

Love
Strength
Wisdom
Abundance
Health

Just after the thought impression is created, try to move your attention out to the 'zone.' If done correctly, you will feel as if you have completely 'forgotten' about the thought that you had just created. Hover in the zone for a few seconds and be aware of the sensations in your body. Repeat five to six times with each word. The whole exercise will take around five minutes.

Notes:

- This exercise will help you to naturally 'drop' a thought by moving your attention to the 'zone.' This is the expert level tactics for letting go of thoughts without the need of an anchor.
- As you become settled in practice, try making the initial thought fainter. Experts can get it to almost a 'pre-thought' level where the thought is so faint that it seems that it is not even created. The purpose of this exercise is to be able to 'spot' the faintest of the cue-thoughts and drop them.

Assignment

Week			
1	2	3	4
✔ 5	6	7	8

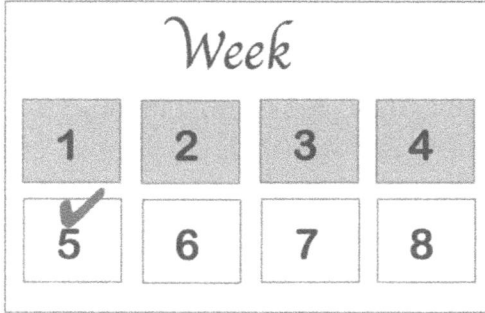

1. Strengthening routines
- Belly breathing (Technique 1): As much as you can.
- Feel the box (Technique 6) before every important meeting and after every work break.
- Mindfully eat (Technique 7), at least four bites in each of your meal.
- Mindfully walk (Technique 8), for at least five minutes every day.
- Every weekend take out 20 minutes and 'watch the judgments' (Technique 9) spanning the key events of the past week that made an impact on your mind. Start with events of today.
- Be watchful of all judgments that you make during day: about people, things and yourself. Do not judge the judgments – just watch and continue with what you were doing (Like the Elephant did in *The Ferret Chronicles*)

Mind-Gym session:

2. Warm-Up
- 10 times bumblebee Humming (Technique 3)
- 20 times balanced breathing (Technique 4)

 3. Core
- Five minutes of sensation watching (Technique 2)
- 10 minutes Hover & Anchor (Technique 5)
- 5 minutes of thought to zone (Technique 10)
- One-minute rest. Close eyes, lean back or lie down.

THINKING OUTSIDE THE BOX

The ability to not engage with the cue-thoughts is the most important aspect of 'cutting holes in the box.' As we build our mind muscles, we will notice more of the 'zone' or the gap between thoughts. These gaps will first appear in Mind-Gym sessions and then they start appearing outside the Gym in our day-to-day life.

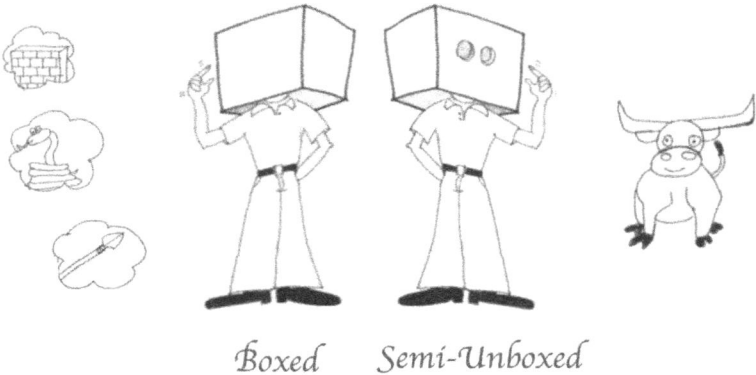

Boxed   *Semi-Unboxed*

These gaps first appear in the quieter moments of the day. And then eventually we will notice them even during the most active part of our lives.

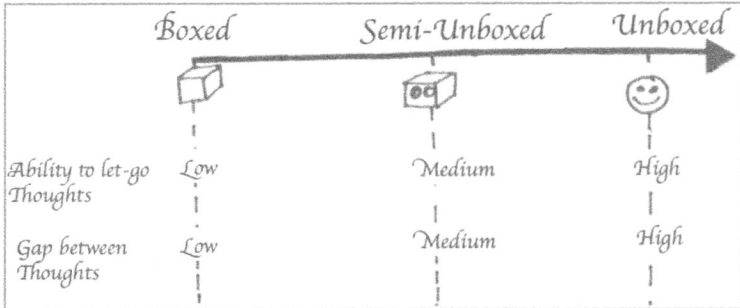

The technique of watching our sensations would enable us to spot our feelings faster than what we used to do earlier. This will give us additional mind muscle power to handle the interruption of cue-thoughts.

We saw in the last chapter that watching cue-thoughts without judging them caused them to dissolve.

We saw that there are *two* ways we can watch the cue-thoughts each linked to one of its components.

First is by observing the image (or mental talk) and second by observing the feeling (via sensations they create).

The *Hover & Anchor* technique should have prepared you to let-go the image heavy cue-thoughts and *Watching Sensations* technique to let-go the sensation heavy ones. If you have followed the gym routines regularly, you will have the skill to perform these effectively on your own.

Whenever you notice an interruption due to a thought dragging you to do something other than what you *want* to do – give attention to the image part of that thought and let it go (using what you learned in the *thought to zone* technique).

If you notice that some feelings have started to arise in your body (they can be positive or negative), sharpen your attention to 'see' the sensation pattern this feeling is causing in the body. Stay with the sensation without judging.

If you do this well, the interrupting thought with its shadow of feeling will diffuse, leaving behind peaceful glow. This works just the same for even so-called negative emotions like fear and jealousy.

If we continue watching thoughts in this way, the gaps between thoughts gradually become more pronounced and one day something magical happens.

You notice that instead of noticing these gaps or the quiet 'zone' come and go between thoughts, you will notice that you are mostly in this mindfulness zone and now thoughts come and go.

The holes in the box are now enduring. You are now Semi-Unboxed.

Signs of Change

"How will I know that I am semi-unboxed?" You ask, " Are there any signs that can help assess this change?"

There are three general indicators that can help you access this change. The degree of these indicators may vary from person to person and the presence of two or more signs is indicative of the clarity level of a semi-unboxed person.

The first sign is the duration of the gap. You will begin to notice that your mind can be *without thoughts*, just observing, for extended periods of time. For a rough reference, you can expect this time to be more than thirty seconds at a time – extending to several minutes. Of course, this is a rough assessment because as soon as you try to observe the duration of your 'not thinking', you will be out of the not-thinking mode.

As a result of this gap, the second sign that you will start to notice will be a *freshness and novelty* even in the most mundane and familiar settings. Do the walls of your bedroom look surprisingly elegant? Does the office window that you have seen through for several years, now frame a beautiful view that you had not noticed earlier? Have the colors become more brilliant? Have smells and taste become more intense? Have you noticed an enhanced appreciation for nature?

The third sign is a newfound sense that your attention now operates on *two distinct tracks*. The feeling, seeing, hearing, tasting and smelling are part of the first track. This familiar track was what we had been relating to primarily when we were in the boxed state. Now a stable second track of attention can be felt. This track of attention is the experiencer of all the feeling, seeing, hearing, tasting and smelling.

This experiencer is felt very distinctly and separate from the experiences.

As you now experience life from the eyehole of the second attention track – the experiencer-track, if we may call it, you start to get a mysterious boost in your creativity.

You have now stepped into the zone of Mindful thinking where less of *Bad thinking* and more of *Good thinking* will come naturally to you.

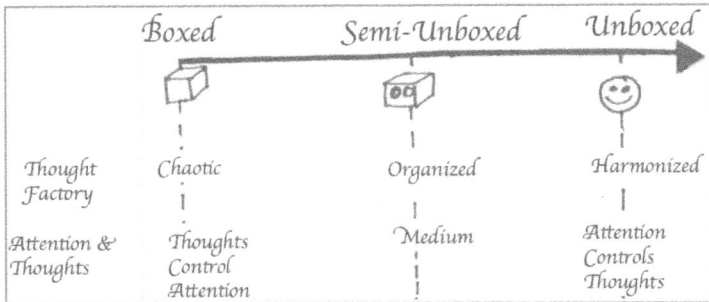

	Boxed	Semi-Unboxed	Unboxed
Thought Factory	Chaotic	Organized	Harmonized
Attention & Thoughts	Thoughts Control Attention	Medium	Attention Controls Thoughts

This growing clarity may lead to some other observable side effects in your life besides the ability to perform Mindful thinking. Try to be aware of these aspects as you continue the unboxing process.

Side Effects of Unboxing

Reduced wired responses.

Eating & Drinking:
Tendency to eat lighter foods.
Tendency to eat smaller and regular meals.
Moderation of indulgences – coffee, tea and alcoholic beverages

Feelings:
Reduced Anger. Reduced Greed. Reduced Fear. Reduced Grief. Reduced Jealousy.
Increased Joy. Increased Gratitude. Increased Love.

Creativity:
Increased creative expression: Painting, Writing, Singing, Dancing, Cooking, Inventions, Unconventional

solutions: Creativity expresses itself through channels that come naturally to you.

The next and final chapter of this book unravels a very subtle mystery in the context of what we have seen and understood thus far - the mysterious I-thought.

I-thought holds the key to the final transformation of the way we think. This transformation happens at *the very moment* we *see* the I-thought.

MIND-GYM SESSION EIGHT

———— ❧ ————

I am hopeful that in the last five weeks you have been able to not only read this book but to also verify the learnings experientially through the exercises and techniques.

These techniques were devised and recommended by masters across ages. These masters wanted to meet you where you were, right at your current level of identification with thoughts, and help liberate your attention. I have just tried to make these exercises more relatable from a contemporary context.

On that note, let's now explore at a technique that is beneficial for those with very active minds. This exercise helps in calming down of thoughts and makes *Hover & Anchor* more efficient. This technique blends breathing, sensation, and attention into one and maneuvers active minds into an aware silence.

Mind-Gym Technique 11: Magical Breath

Sit comfortably in an upright position. Close eyes and do belly breathing for one minute.

Now put your attention on the sensations in your back, specifically around your spine. Move the attention from the bottom of the spine to top of your neck your neck and back down.

Now synchronize this up and down movement with belly breathing. Move your attention up slowly as you breathe in. Move it down along the back as you breathe out.

Repeat twenty times.

Notes:

- You may feel faint tingling sensations along your spine as you trace your attention up and down.
- This exercise will be done before Hover & Anchor, as a warm-up. It settles down the thoughts further, making Hover & Anchor more effective.

Once you have a stable Mind-Gym routine, you will notice a marked difference in your ability to let-go of cue-thoughts during your daily life. And if you want, you can transform many day-to-day activities into a Mind-Gym session.

Mind-Gym Bonus: So many Anchors!

You can play with many interesting anchor options. These are not substitutes of our core exercise of *Hover & Anchor* but can supplement it.

Perform a few repetitions of moving your attention from whatever you are doing or thinking to these new anchors.

Just remember that the basic principle is to move the attention back to the anchor when you realize it is wandering into thoughts.

1. While sitting, pay attention to the pressure on your buttocks. Balance the weight evenly. Now use the attention of this balance as an anchor. Do a few repetitions of moving your attention from whatever you are doing or thinking, back to the feeling of this balanced weight.

Similarly:

2. Move your attention to the tip of your nose.
3. Move your attention to your breath.
4. Move your attention to any pain in your body.

---

5. Move your attention to a flickering flame or fire.

6. Move your attention to a fading sound.

7. Move your attention to a stringed instrument.

8. Move your attention to the sky.

9. Move your attention to the taste of what you are eating or drinking.

Note: There are also some *expert level* techniques that point your attention to the 'zone' directly, bypassing the anchor. *Thought to zone* is one such technique. We will explore one more in next chapter.

Assignment (Week 6 and beyond)

1. Strengthening routines
-   Breathe from your belly.
-   Eat and walk mindfully.
-   Be watchful of all judgments: about people, things and yourself. Do not judge the judgments – just watch and continue with what you were doing.
-   On every weekend, take out 20 minutes to perform *watching the judgments* exercise spanning the key events of the past week that made an impact on your mind. Start with events of today, moving back through previous days.
-   Feel the Box before every important meeting and after every work break.

Mind-Gym session:

These will be ideally twice a day sessions. Minimally once a day.

2. Warm-Up
- 10 times bumblebee Humming (Technique 3)
- 20 times balanced breathing (Technique 4)
- 20 times magical breath (Technique 11)

3. Core
- Five minutes of sensation watching (Technique 2)
- 15 minutes Hover & Anchor (Technique 5). (You can increase the duration to 20 minutes if you want to but not more than that)
- 5 minutes of thought to zone (Technique 10)
- One-minute rest. Close eyes, lean back or lie down.

WHERE IS THE THINKER?

W e have covered many aspects about the thought-factory so far. We have seen that cue-thought is a cleverly encoded judgment. This judgment summarizes an experience from our past into two paired components - an image and a feeling.

The image and the bundle of sensations then act as a cue for a person to respond to the current situation. The cue points us to a thought weaver, which then creates the action-thoughts required to handle the situation at hand. Actions then follow these action-thoughts.

We also explored the fact that we have acquired a collection of thought weavers from across the ages. These weavers can spin out pre-programmed stories through a hard-wired response.

There is one more thing in this thought-factory that we have not covered so far. This thing is one of the most mysterious and intriguing aspects of the thought-factory. This is the *third type of thought* in the factory beside cue and action-thoughts. This thought is known as the I-thought.

The 'I-thought'

We know that cue-thought has a visual or image and a feeling encoded in it. There is one more piece of (implicit) information in the cue that we will now explore. This piece is related to the I-thought.

We know that contained within the cue-thought is verdict or summary of a judgment. The 'feeling' or emotion in the thought was your response to a particular situation in the past. The past situation is summarized by a visual - the image. The past feeling is then evoked to capture your attention and influence your actions if you face a similar situation.

Isn't this mechanism somewhat similar to how the courts look for previous judgments in order to guide current judgments?

In case of the thought-factory, however, this guidance comes unsolicited, and some of these judgments come from unknown sources, from times when we were still riding on camels. Some are even older from the time we just got down from the trees to explore the savanna. These judgments are due to cue-thoughts that we have inherited much the same way animals with primitive thinking learn from their previous generations.

Since our current judgments are influenced by these older judgments, it would be perhaps worthwhile to find out about *who is this mysterious judge*, whose judgments we carry in the fabric of our body-mind in the form of cue-thoughts?

But how do I find out more about this Judge?

"Easy," you may say, "Since all these Judgments are a summary of how the judge felt like in a situation, you can just review these individual judgments and get an idea of the personality of the judge. Well, you may not exactly see him or her but you can deduce a lot about the judges personality."

Bingo! I applaud your assessment. "How about you show me how this works with an example?" I ask pulling out an old book, pointing at a page, containing a collection of cue-thoughts belonging to a person from 500 BC. "Be careful, this page is ancient."

You look at the tattered yellow page and squint your eyes as you skim through the collection of cue-thoughts - through each image and feeling that was recorded in the past.

"I see a familiar pattern", you frown in concentration," A lot of these cue-thoughts have an image of a fruit in their visual. Different type of fruits. This person used to judge fruits?" you mumble as you sift through the cues again, "And I also see a consistent feeling of dislike, repulsion, hate across all these cue-thoughts ...", your eyes brighten up.

"Therefore I can conclude that this particular Judge *did not like fruits*!" you flash a smile.

Then going through several others of judgments, made by this person from the past, you build a rich profile of the Judge. What he likes, dislikes loves craves for, etc.

"The Judge's profile and personality can be inferred from all these judgments!" you smile at me "Elementary, dear Watson!"

"Great," I smile *Now show me that Judge!"*

"There is no judge I can show you" you seem puzzled at my question "we are inferring the personality of the Judge from the judgments here... " You say raising your eyebrows.

"So I can see the judgments – but not the Judge?" I remain persistent in my queries.

"These judgments are from past. How can I show you the original judge? The judge is inferred. All that remain at this moment are the judgments – in the form of the thought impressions that we see here", you say pointing at the document.

"So there are *real* judgments, but a *virtual* Judge?"

There is *no Judge*?

"How about the judgments that *I* created. Ones I am sure that were made by me, like this one", you ask pointing to a cue-thought that was created when a spider crawled on your legs when you were four years old. The cue-thought had a visual of very scary looking spider and a feeling of fear.

"That four-year-old who made the judgment about the spider is also not here anymore? Is he?" I ask.

"Hmmm maybe not ..." You nod.

"The person who created that thought is not you anymore." I encourage you to explore this fact further and respond from a place of clarity without the influence of cue-thoughts.

"I am a thirty year old who is rationally convinced about my fear of spiders", you respond after a long pause, "The judgment from a four-year-old is now part of my personality. That judgment still plays an important part in my present. And this is just one of the numerous past judgments that has shaped my current actions. These cue-thoughts make up my personality!" you beam as you see through the mechanism that created this illusion!

The entity that I had assumed as 'me' was inferred from all these cue-thought judgments. New verdicts, especially the stronger ones reinforced this impression as I continued to believe that this 'Judge' was a real personality when in fact it was just a concept. There was no Judge. Just judgments.

Stored over the ages, older judgments had influenced recent ones – many times erroneously. The judgments gradually began to reinforce a pattern and then *the pattern itself overrode the utility of the judgment.*

My attention then started to believe that the imaginary judge, inferred from the bundle of cue-thoughts, was "*Me*."

This virtual judge became my projected personality as well as an autonomous independent entity responding to cues and feedbacks.

This personality filters the things that I can see. I can only see things that are approved by and conform to the judgments that created this virtual personality.

We just assume that the personality exists because information about past judgments exist. *In reality, there is no Judge. There are only records of past judgments.*

These judgments reinforce and sustain the Judge, which now creates new judgments – creating a loop that sustains the illusion. Let's call this virtual judge the "I-thought." So I-thought or the Judge remains implicitly embedded in cue-thoughts.

It is like a virtual thread that ties together the beads of cue-thought - a bunch of judgments over a lifetime.

But the thread itself is imaginary. The stack of thoughts creates the illusion of the Judge, personality or the I-thought. *And the moment we 'see' this fact, the thread disintegrates.* And with this thread gone – the stack of cue-thoughts fall apart.

> **We all can evolve the way we think at this very moment if we truly understand this trick**

The cue-thoughts that were up until now held together by this illusory thread which kept together a bunch of judgments - ancient, old and new – those cues now scatter and float around in thin air!

The cues do not disappear but your attention is not attracted to their story anymore. It can now see the world that these thoughts had been obscuring when they had assembled in form of a box.

Now there is a quality of ease and natural non-judgment in your attention that makes you see the rivers and mountains in their true glory.

Another important realization in this state is the feeling of gratitude, love, and connectedness with the world.

You are now Unboxed!

Remember that the cue-thoughts are still around in the thought-factory and will continue to serve content based on past-unresolved judgments. But now, their ability to attract your attention will be significantly reduced.

The unboxed continue watching these impressions; they keep 'watching the thoughts' with their images and sensations, without judging them and thus without creating additional impressions.

The harmonized thought-factory now spins out impactful and efficient action-thoughts and actions that are not limited by the uncontrolled cue-thoughts.

> In the unboxed state, thoughts no longer control your actions. You control the thoughts and use them to drive creative and impactful actions.

Here you are naturally inclined to perform more of *Good thinking* and less Bad thinking harnessing *the power of Mindful Thinking.*

With mindful thinking, you make fewer mistakes. Your attention does not get easily distracted. You can do things that you want to do much better and quicker. You become more creative, spinning out cool things that surprise everyone – including you. You also make more friends - many, many of them.

In this state, peace and harmony play with creativity and compassion, creating a joyous dance of life every human was born to experience.

MIND-GYM SESSION NINE

This session requires an ability to observe and 'let-go' thoughts. We do not want to perform these exercises when the attention is not yet stable enough to deal with cue-thoughts.

You can follow the three practical tests to assess if you are ready (which are basically the signs of the semi-unboxed state): (1) extended periods without thoughts, (2) noticing yet unseen beauty in things around you and (3) the awareness of the second track of attention – the track that *watches* all your experiences.

This is the trick we have been trying to understand all the while – the spectacular fact of the missing judge.

All we will need now is to rely on our deepest intuition, relax, and make these inquiries.

"For how long?" you may ask.

As long as it takes. And you will not regret it!

Mind-Gym Exercise 1: Who are you?

This is a thought exercise.

Magical time-travelling creatures have invaded earth and taken it over. These creatively cruel beings want to torment us. They have ordered every person to hand over the decisions relating to the remaining part of their life to a person from their past.

You will need to time travel to meet this person and get written instructions from this person. You will then need to follow the instructions for the remaining part of your life.

You, very cleverly appoint your past self for this assignment (who wants to give control of your life to *others* after all!).

Which "past you" will you choose to hand over your remaining life to? You will need to choose a specific year. Can you reflect on your past and appoint the wisest *you* who can now be in charge of the rest of your life?

Notes:

- How comfortable are you doing this? Would you rather *not do this* if you had a choice?
- How comfortable are you in basing your current decisions on past judgments? Imagine yourself as a five-year-old. Ten? Fifteen? Did you cringe? But aren't we doing this? Our past judgments influence us each day via cue-thoughts we had created in the past.
- Knowing well that our current judgments are colored by past judgments – if you have to create an image of yourself with due acknowledgment to all the past contributors, how will this personality look like?

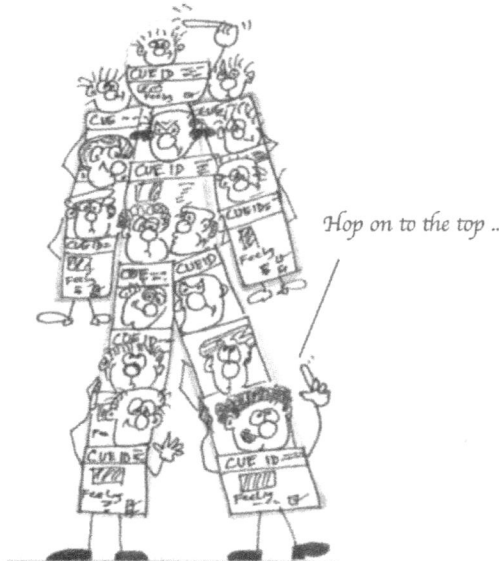

Hop on to the top ..

Mind-Gym Technique 12: Where are you?

Sit comfortably in an upright position. Close your eyes and belly breathe for one minute.

Now put your attention on the sensations of your entire body.

"Who is feeling the sensations?"

For most, this will be the second track of attention - the witness that observes the thoughts and actions.

The next part of this technique is to ask yourself "*Where* is this second track of attention operating from? Where is its center?"

Use your attention to scan everything that it can. Where is this watcher of the experiences, physically? You do not want to make any intellectual concepts about this question. It is as simple as pointing to the exact location where this experiencer judge resides.

It is important that you perform this inquiry when you are at ease and not guarded.

And do not expect any outcome.

You can make this inquiry during any quiet pause in your day and as many times you want.

Notes:

- If you get tempted to point to a location like head or between your eyebrows etc. – try to feel that location with full attention. Is the second track of attention, the watcher, *really* located in that place? Is that *really* the 'center' from which it is active?

I will, of course, not reveal the answer to this inquiry. I am sure you find the answer on your own. Just relax and follow your intuition!

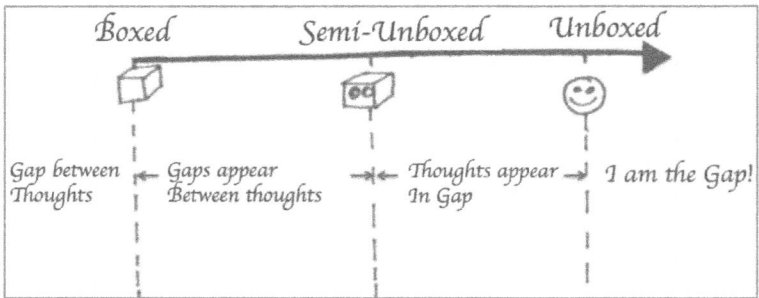

Boxed	*Semi-Unboxed*	*Unboxed*
Gap between Thoughts	Gaps appear Between thoughts	Thoughts appear In Gap	I am the Gap!

A 'relaxed nondoing' will eventually reveal the answer to this enquiry. The attention that progressed from being aware of the gap or 'zone' more and more, now realizes a yet another amazing thing – that *I am the gap*.

"What does that mean?" you might ask, "*being the gap?*"

You will get your answer when *your* awareness rests in the zone stripped of the illusion of I-thought.

Of course, there is much more to explore in the magical inner-world than what we have covered in this book. But now you know the key tools to get you started in that incredible journey.

So keep Mind-Gymming - and when you are ready for the next level of exploration, be assured that you will have a guide to help you.

And this guide is within you.

THE INNER GUIDE

"The coming of the kingdom of God is not something that can be observed, nor will people say, 'Here it is,' or 'There it is,' because the kingdom of God is in your midst."

— Jesus Christ (*Luke 17: 20-37*)

"The settling down of the ripples of the mind is Yoga. Then the seer rests in its true nature.

At other times the seer is identified with the ripples"

— Patanjali (*Yoga Sutra: Verse 2*)

"Our life is shaped by our mind. We become what we think.

Suffering follows an evil thought as wheels of a cart follow the oxen that draw it"

— Buddha (*Dhammapada: Verse 1*)

∼∼∼

"O traveler, if you are in search of That

Don't look outside, look inside yourself and seek That!"

— Jalaluddin Rumi.

∼∼∼

"One who knows other people is wise.

One who knows himself is enlightened"

— Lao Tzu (*Tao Te Ching*)

∼∼∼

"Now, if we see the truth of that - that the thinker is thought, that there is no thinker separate from thought, but only the process of thinking - , then what happens?"

— J. Krishnamurti

AFTERWORD

With the recent advent of web-based information, that's now ubiquitous via smartphones and social media, our thought factories are indeed going through a major overhaul.

A lot of the things our brains used to perform in the past have now been automated – so we should have expected to have more time at hand to do things we like. Unfortunately, things have not turned out to be so. With an ever-decreasing attention span that is being continuously challenged by a plethora of smartphone apps, our thought-factory is now even more susceptible to random cue-thoughts.

Therefore I strongly feel that we are living in a time when mindfulness related teachings are needed more than ever. Especially the ones that are on *application of mindfulness* in our day-to-day life. This age-old wisdom and lessons need to be adapted so that the new generation can relate to them. This book is a small contribution to that effort.

The techniques included in this book are all tried and tested ones that have worked across the ages. They have also worked for me and also of the individuals I have coached and guided.

Main Sources

The techniques used in this book are based on two important and somewhat related schools that help us see through the illusions created by our mind: Yoga (as described by Maharishi Patanjali) and Dhamma (as described by Shakyamuni Buddha).

The primary focus of the exercises that were put together in this book is to help our attention to 'let – go' of distracting subconscious triggers. These cue-thought triggers or sanskaras have been covered in both of the schools and both stress on building up the ability to 'watch' the influences of these cues as they appear in our body and minds.

The mind-Gym techniques draw upon the breathing exercises (Pranayama), meditation (Dhyana) and the practice of Samayama as explained in the Yoga Sutra. These methods are designed to settle down the ripples of the mind, which is the primary objective of Yoga. The more known aspect of Yoga, postures or

Asanas, are not covered in these techniques, but if you already have a practice that includes them, they would naturally compliment the mind-Gym exercises.

The feeling and sensation related methods are based on the four levels of *watching* explained in Buddha's Mahāsatipaṭṭhāna Sutta, which enables Vipassana or seeing things as they are.

Thoughts & More Thoughts

The techniques in the book have a simple objective – *to help our attention get out of the lure of uncontrolled thoughts* and therefore discover it's real expansive nature. This expanded attention is also known as awareness and beyond that; consciousness.

With the advent of digital age and digital distractions, our engagement with thoughts has grown exponentially. I, for one, have experienced this first hand as would have most of you. This is why *thought based* techniques were given more importance in this compilation, including anchor-thought based meditation (Dhyana) and the thought-to-zone (Samayama) practice that can help build our ability to let go the cue-thought distractions in day-to-day life.

The Basics

This book intends to give its readers – especially the tech-savvy younger readers the basics about applied-mindfulness or how mindfulness can be *applied* to day-to-day life.

Therefore one of my key objectives was to provide the 'big picture' with an optimal level of simplification that can get one started. Of course, there is much more to uncover in the wonderful world of expanded attention or awareness, but these exercises should be enough to get you started on that.

The Enquiry

The chapter on I-thought, is based on techniques that were put forth by Shri Ramana Maharishi. This method of self-enquiry has become popular in recent times, particularly in the West. My advice, which draws on my personal experience, is that this method is most effective after one is semi-unboxed and has a stable degree of witness.

And when this watching of feelings and thoughts happens naturally and effortlessly, that is the only technique that one would need.

The purpose of this book is to guide you towards that natural state that remains accessible to all of us.

Further Reading

For those who want to explore the path of unboxing further, here are some of my favorite readings:

Stories & Fables
The Alchemist by Paulo Coelho
The Little Prince by Antoine de Saint-Exupéry
Jonathan Livingston Seagull by Richard Bach
Illusions by Richard Bach

Unboxed Living
Tao of Leadership by John Heider
Living in Simplicity by multiple authors

Thinking & Thoughts:
On Mind and Thought by J Krishnamurthy
Power of Now by Ekhart Tolle
Happiness Beyond Thought by Gary Weber
The Story of Philosophy by Will Durant

Watching Thoughts:
To be Human by J Krishnamurthy
The Dhammapada by Eknath Easwaran
New Earth by Ekhart Tolle

Mental Chatter & Default Mode Network
Functional-Anatomic Fractionation of the Brain's Default Network by Jessica R. Andrews-Hanna, Jay S. Reidler, Jorge Sepulcre, Renee Poulin, and Randy L. Buckner
Meditation leads to reduced default mode network activity beyond an active task by Kathleen A. Garrison, Thomas A. Zeffiro, Dustin Scheinost, R. Todd Constable, and Judson A. Brewer

Techniques & Exercises
Deep Meditation by Yogani
Samayama by Yogani
Light on Pranayama by BVK Iyengar
The Heart of Yoga by TKV Desikachar
The Book of Secrets: 112 techniques of Meditation by Osho
The Science of Being & the Art of Living by Mahesh Yogi
Art of Living: Vipassana Meditation by SN Goenka
A Systematic Course in the Yoga and Kriya by Swami
Satyananda Saraswati
Who am I by Ramana Maharishi

About the Box & Beyond
Yoga Sutra by Patanjali: Commentary & Translations.
  -   Yoga the Alpha and the Omega: by Osho
  -   Raj Yoga & Patanjali's Yoga Aphorisms: by Swami
      Vivekananda
Satipaṭṭhāna: The Direct Path to Realization by Anālayo

ACKNOWLEDGEMENTS

This book started out as a companion booklet for a magic realism based spiritual fiction novel that I had written to convey the message about cue-thoughts and the troubles they could create.

As I started compiling the techniques and exercises, the project took a life of it's own. I felt compelled to summarize the core practices that had guided the seekers of mindfulness across ages. I thank all these masters with my deepest gratitude, especially Yogani, who has anonymously coached thousands of seekers through his site on Advanced Yoga Practices at aypsite.org, helping them find the guide within.

I was surprised by the simplicity of the core teaching about how to trick the mind to get out of the control of thoughts. But complex dynamics in the outer-world had somehow obscured this message through millenniums.

To map the dynamics of the inner-world, I drew upon the learnings from my teachers at MIT. I thank all my teachers and guides at Massachusetts Institute of Technology who coached me on Systems Thinking, an approach that uses the *big picture view* to address complex problems.

I would like to thank Kevin Martin, author of *Perceive This* for introducing the exercise to explore the nature of attention in Unbox! workshops. I want to thank Dr. Gary Weber, author of *Happiness Beyond Thoughts* (and several others) for introducing me to the world of Default Mode Network that helped me relate the Unbox! narrative with recent studies in Neuroscience.

I also want to thank the cartoonists of MAD magazine, especially the maddest of them all - Don Martin, who inspired me to start cartooning when I was a teenager. I intend to continue to share insights from the traditionally somber inner-world in a cheerful way through humorous illustrations through my upcoming books and also through my cartoon blog at thoughtUnboxed.com.

I want to thank my writing coach, friend and bestselling author Rachna for her continued guidance as she patiently catalyzes the metamorphosis of a nerd into a writer.

The publication team, Jyotsana and Sushmitha for cover design, book design and Amazon & create space publishing help. Ros Webb, for the cover illustration.

Vandana for her earnest feedbacks across several revisions and for generally being there. Nisheeth, for his fantastic and diligent review and critique of the content and his patient prodding. Salil for his strategic comments and keeping me honest. Sonali, for peer reviewing the inner-world content and giving her valuable feedbacks on the sensation techniques. Monideepa for her helpful advice on how to align the content for the younger audience. Saty for his recommendation to focus on core techniques & insights. Gopal for his practical viewpoint about winning without a race and Irina for her extremely valuable feedback that helped frame the revised edition.

My young millennial reviewers Siddhant and Samay who helped in keeping the message simple. Tanya for her assistance in the illustrations. My brother Devraj and my dear wife Anisha, my biggest critics who kept me focused through the several revisions.

Mummy, for getting me started in the path of Yoga. And Baban and Mum for everything.

ABOUT THE AUTHOR

Prithvi Raj Banerjee is a Boston-based, Indian Institute of Technology & Massachusetts Institute of Technology (MIT) educated technologist, entrepreneur and writer.

He is also a Yoga and mindfulness coach and has trained under masters from celebrated spiritual traditions in the world.

He is the founder of the MindGym Initiative, a non-profit focused on creating awareness about mindful thinking amongst the younger generation.

Prithvi has co-founded two technology startups. An avid traveler, he shuttles around the globe with his college sweetheart & wife of 22 years, and their two lovely kids.

His upcoming novel 'Kālī' is a magical realism based spiritual fiction that demystifies the mechanisms that have conditioned the human mind through a gripping story that has a blend of historical fiction, adventure, and mysticism with an underlying humorous style.

www.ingramcontent.com/pod-product-compliance
Lightning Source LLC
Chambersburg PA
CBHW030416100426

42812CB00028B/2983/J